window on
cyprus

P.I.O. 315/2010 – 8.000
ISBN 978-9963-38-770-0

Published by the Press and Information Office,
Republic of Cyprus
www.moi.gov.cy/pio

Third Edition

Editorial Supervision and Coordination: Miltos Miltiadou
Editors: Andreas Lyritsas
Polly Lyssiotis
Angeliki Nicolaidou Mavrommati
Michalis Michael
Editorial Assistance: Maria Georgiou
Photography Editor: Yiannos Miltiadou

Designed by: Andreas Georgiou
Cover by: Christos Avraamides
Printed by: Eptalofos S.A., Athens

CREDITS

The Press and Information Office, publishers of the book,
express their appreciation and gratitude to all the individuals,
agencies and organizations that have contributed to the
realization of this project. Special thanks go to those who have
kindly contributed essays and photographs for the book.

Text: Much of the text has been prepared or adapted by
the editorial team from other publications of the Press and
Information Office. Some segments represent contributions
by other government agencies. A number of essays
represent contributions by experts, who kindly extended their
cooperation for this project. They are cited in the book under
the title of their respective contribution. Their assistance is
greatly valued. Our thanks also to Mr Leonidas Malenis for his
kind permission to use his poem "Gold-green leaf".

Photography: The majority of the photographs used in
the book come from the photographic archive of the Press
and Information Office. In addition, a number of institutions
and individuals have generously given their permission for
the use of photographs in the book. They are listed below
in recognition of their kind cooperation, which is greatly
appreciated.

Agencies and Organisations
Agricultural Research Institute
Archaelogical Museum of Cyprus
Central Bank of Cyprus
Cultural Foundation
Cultural Services, Ministry of Education and Culture
Cyprus Olympic Committee
Cyprus Ports Authority
Cyprus Telecommunications Authority
Cyprus Theatre Organisation Archive
Cyprus Tourism Organisation
Cyprus Wine Museum
Department of Agriculture
Department of Merchant Shipping
Department of Postal Services
Department of Town Planning and Housing
Electricity Authority of Cyprus
En Tipis Publications
European Commission
Leventis Municipal Museum of Nicosia
Nicosia Municipal Arts Centre
Press and Information Office
Public Works Department
State General Laboratory
Theatro Ena
Theatro Scala
United Nations
Water Development Department

Individuals

Avraamides Christos
Charalambous Constantinos
Christodoulou Katia
Coutas Andreas
Demetriou Costas
Farmakas Antonis
Ioannides Takis
Kokkinias Panos

Lazanitis Andreas
Louka Nikos
Panayides Christos
Panztis Andreas
Photo Larkos
Vatiliotis George
Violaris Christos
Zafiriou Lefkios

CONTENTS

ΧΡΟΝΙΑ ΚΥΠΡΙΑΚΗ ΔΗΜΟΚΡΑΤΙΑ
YIL KIBRIS CUMHURİYETİ

A Message from the President of the Republic of Cyprus
H.E. Mr Demetris Christofias

In 2010 Cyprus proudly celebrates its fiftieth anniversary as an independent state. The anniversary marks the appearance and the modern historical course of our country and our people. It marks our successes and accomplishments but also the tragedies our country has experienced during the fifty years of its existence. The Republic of Cyprus marks half a century of life but its territory and people unfortunately remain divided by the force of arms. Understandably, this tragic development casts a sad shadow over the joyful fiftieth independence anniversary.

In 1960 Cyprus gained its independence and joined the family of nations officially as the Republic of Cyprus, after a protracted and hard anti-colonial struggle by our people to win the right to self-determination. Since winning their independence, it became necessary for our people to undertake new hard struggles to defend it, and to defend the sovereignty, the freedom and the territorial integrity of our country.

The Republic of Cyprus faced many problems during the first years of its existence: problems in the functioning of the state, but also problems resulting from foreign interference in the domestic affairs of our country. The divisive elements that were incorporated in the Zurich-London agreements, which were imposed on the people of Cyprus, but also the activities of extremist elements, fuelled the clashes between the two communities on Cyprus, the Greek Cypriot and the Turkish Cypriot, that had lived together on the island in peace for centuries.

The clashes were the antecedents of the great tragedy that our people experienced in 1974, and which was brought about by a twofold crime against our country: The coup carried out by the junta of Athens and the terrorist organization of EOKA B', and the illegal invasion and occupation of a large part of the territory of the Republic of Cyprus by Turkey. Our people still suffer the tragic consequences of the Turkish occupation to this day.

Our firm goal remains the achievement of a peaceful settlement to the Cyprus problem so that the occupation and the colonization are terminated and Cyprus is reunited. This can be feasible in the context

of a functional and viable bizonal, bicommunal federation that restores and safeguards the human rights and basic freedoms of all the people of Cyprus and which makes Cyprus, again, the common homeland for the Greek Cypriots and the Turkish Cypriots.

The Republic of Cyprus has shown remarkable resilience over time and we are rightly proud for the great progress that has been achieved in all spheres of life in our country.

The great progress that has been accomplished is clearly chronicled through the pages of the book "Window on Cyprus." Our country has been transformed from a poor, underdeveloped island, into a modern, thriving democracy, a respected member of the international community and an energetic and equal member of the European Union. Independence was the great platform that enabled us to progress and advance as a country and as a people in spite of the tragedies and the problems that have piled up as a result of the occupation by Turkey.

As we honour the independence anniversary, we pay tribute to all those who made sacrifices for the liberation of our country, in defense of its independence as well as for the protection and strengthening of its democratic institutions. Drawing the right lessons from the hardships we have experienced and the mistakes we have made, we continue the struggle and the effort with optimism and determination in order to meet the challenges and the demands of our time and to move Cyprus forward.

On the occasion of the fiftieth anniversary of the Republic of Cyprus, I convey my warmest congratulations and my best wishes to all the citizens: Greek Cypriots, Turkish Cypriots, Armenians, Latins and Maronites. We are committed to carry on the struggle to reunite Cyprus and to transform it into an island of everlasting peace and prosperity for all our people.

The Gymnasium at the ancient city-kingdom of Salamis.

history

CYPRUS IN HISTORY

The history of Cyprus is one of the oldest recorded in the world. From the earliest times, Cyprus' historical significance far outweighed its small size. Its strategic position at the crossroads of three continents and its considerable resources of copper and timber combined to make it a highly desirable territorial acquisition.

> The history of Cyprus is one of the oldest recorded in the world. The first signs of life date to the tenth millennium BC.

The first signs of life date to the tenth millennium BC (Pre-Neolithic age), but it was the discovery of copper (3900 - 2500 BC) that was to bring wealth and trade to the island. Around 1200 BC, a process began that was to largely mark the island with the predominant national identity that it still has today; the arrival of Mycenaean-Achaean Greeks as permanent settlers, who brought with them their language and culture.

Cyprus was subsequently subjugated by various conquerors; nevertheless, it managed to retain its Greek identity. The Turkish Cypriots came much later, as a result of the Ottoman occupation of the island for more than three hundred years (1571-1878), and have contributed their own heritage to the country.

Protome of a cat made of andesite from Pareklisia-"Shyllourokambos", tenth millennium BC.

NEOLITHIC PERIOD (8200 - 3900 BC)

Remains of the oldest known settlements in Cyprus date from this period. They can best be seen at Khirokitia, just off the Nicosia to Limassol highway. The use of carbon-14 dating method proved that life in the settlement of Khirokitia started in the sixth millennium BC, indicating that Cyprus was inhabited during the same period as Mesopotamia and Greece. However, a more recent dating procedure suggests that the settlement might even date back to the eighth millennium BC.

At first, only stone vessels were used. Pottery appeared in a second phase after 5000 BC. Idols of clay or stone representing human and animal figures are the earliest specimens of Cypriot sculpture.

Diabase stone anthropomorphic figurine from Khirokitia, Neolithic Period, 7000-6000 BC.

Necklace of dentalium bead shells and precious stones from the Aceramic Neolithic settlement of Khirokitia, c. 6500 BC.

11

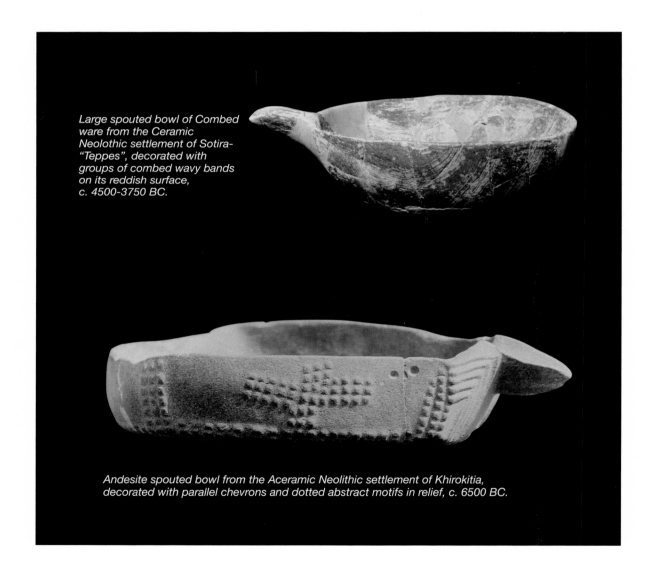

Large spouted bowl of Combed ware from the Ceramic Neolothic settlement of Sotira-"Teppes", decorated with groups of combed wavy bands on its reddish surface, c. 4500-3750 BC.

Andesite spouted bowl from the Aceramic Neolithic settlement of Khirokitia, decorated with parallel chevrons and dotted abstract motifs in relief, c. 6500 BC.

Part of the Aceramic Neolithic settlement at Khirokitia, c. 7000-6000 BC.

CHALCOLITHIC AGE (3900 - 2500 BC)

A transitional period between the Stone Age and the Bronze Age. Most Chalcolithic settlements were found in southwestern Cyprus where a fertility cult developed. During this period there were changes in many fields. The burial customs of the Cypriots changed and the deceased were now buried in separate cemeteries. Several clay figurines representing the goddess of fertility were produced. New forms in pottery were introduced and new styles in decoration appeared. Copper was discovered and was beginning to be exploited on a small scale.

Clay bowl with three long feet of the developed Red-on-White ware from the Chalcolithic II settlement of Ambelikou-"Ayios Georghios" decorated with linear geometric designs on its whitish surface, c. 2700 BC.

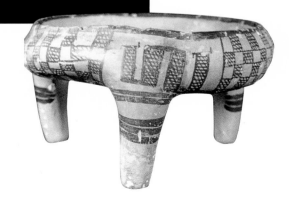

Female limestone figurine from Lemba, Chalcolithic Period, c. 2500 BC.

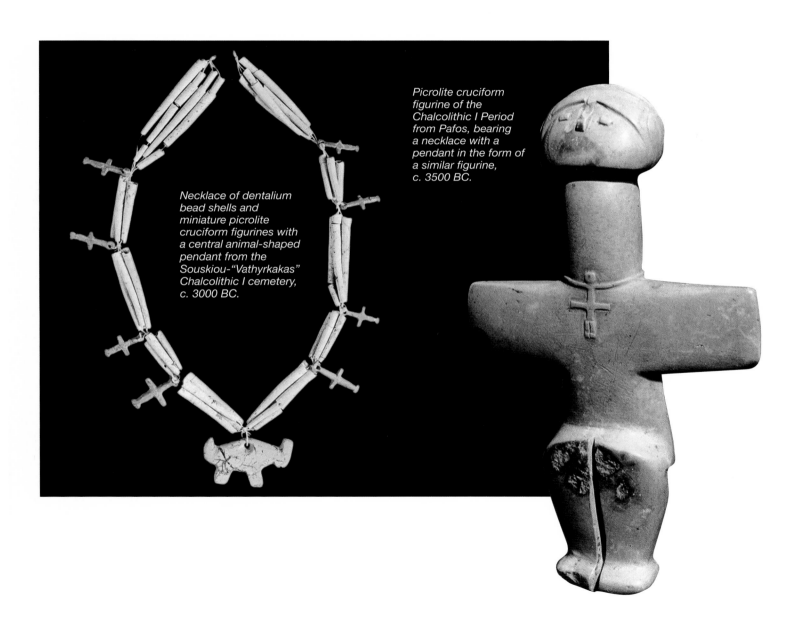

Picrolite cruciform figurine of the Chalcolithic I Period from Pafos, bearing a necklace with a pendant in the form of a similar figurine, c. 3500 BC.

Necklace of dentalium bead shells and miniature picrolite cruciform figurines with a central animal-shaped pendant from the Souskiou-"Vathyrkakas" Chalcolithic I cemetery, c. 3000 BC.

15

BRONZE AGE (2500 - 1050 BC)

The most significant event during this period was the extensive exploitation of copper mines on the island bringing wealth to Cyprus. Gradually, copper mixed with tin produced a much harder material called bronze, the discovery of which dramatically boosted the island's economy and commerce. Trade developed with the Near East, Egypt and the Aegean where Cyprus was known under the name of Alasia.

> Around 1200 BC, mass waves of Achaean Greeks came to settle on the island and established the first city-kingdoms of Pafos, Salamis, Kition and Kourion.

After 1400 BC, Mycenaeans from Greece first came to the island as merchants. Around 1200 BC, mass waves of Achaean Greeks came to settle on the island and established the first city-kingdoms of Pafos, Salamis, Kition and Kourion, spreading the Greek language, religion and customs. The hellenisation of the island was then in progress.

Early Bronze Age composite ritual vase of Red Polished ware from Pellapais - "Vounous" consisting of one main jug with a long cylindrical neck and seven smaller jugs, attached and communicating to each other, c.2200-2000 BC.

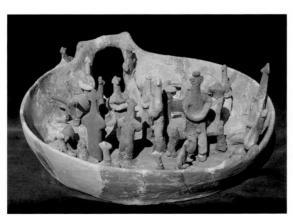

Clay model of an open-air circular sanctuary of the Early Bronze Age from Pellapais-"Vounous" enclosing groups of human figures, participating in a certain ceremony, and bulls leaded led for sacrifice in honour of the divinities depicted in relief against the wall of the sanctuary, holding snakes and wearing bulls´ masks, the symbols of the Fertility goddess and the Death divinity, c. 2500-2300 BC.

Middle Bronze Age jug of White Painted ware from a tomb at Lapithos, with cut away neck, standing figures on shoulder and elegant rich, linear, decoration in black paint all over its surface, c. 1750 BC.

16

Bronze stand from Kourion with four legs, supporting a ring, and decoration of four human figures in panels in front of the "sacred tree", three standing and carrying fish and a bronze ingot on their shoulders and one seated and playing her lyre, c. 1200 BC, British Museum, London.

Bronze statue of the Horned God from Enkomi, Late Bronze Age 1200 - 1150 BC.

Red and Black Polished clay bowls, Early Bronze Age from Vounous.

17

Ivory mirror handle from a tomb at Palaepafos, with decoration of incised patterns and a composition of a warrior in relief, stabbing a lion with a dagger and resembling the mythological scene of Hercules killing the Nemean Lion, c. 1200 BC.

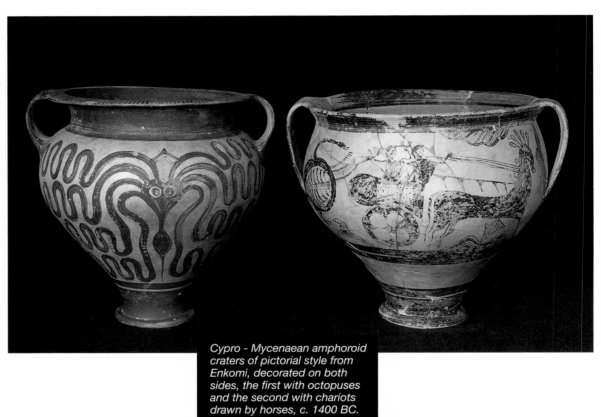

Cypro - Mycenaean amphoroid craters of pictorial style from Enkomi, decorated on both sides, the first with octopuses and the second with chariots drawn by horses, c. 1400 BC.

18

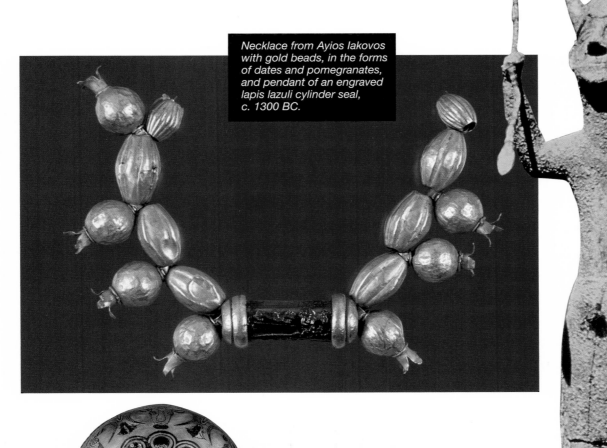

Necklace from Ayios Iakovos with gold beads, in the forms of dates and pomegranates, and pendant of an engraved lapis lazuli cylinder seal, c. 1300 BC.

Bronze statuette of the "Ingot God", the god protector of the Cypriot copper mines, from his sanctuary at Enkomi, standing on a copper ingot and armed with a horned helmet, shield and spear, c. 1200 BC.

Silver bowl from Enkomi, with embossed decoration of bull's heads, rosettes and lotus flowers in gold and niello, c. 1400-1350 BC.

GEOMETRIC PERIOD (1050 - 750 BC)

During the Iron Age, which is also called Cypro-Geometric period, Cyprus had ten Greek city-kingdoms, and the cult of goddess Aphrodite flourished on the island. Phoenicians settled at Kition in the ninth century BC and then extended their influence over a large part of the island. This important political event had a primary influence on the art and culture of Cyprus. An oriental taste in the art and crafts was introduced and the first Phoenician imports appeared on the island. The eighth century BC was a period of great prosperity.

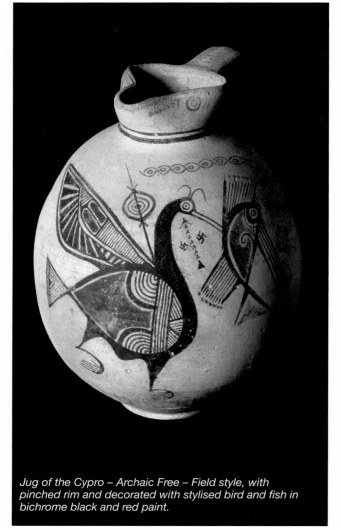

Jug of the Cypro – Archaic Free – Field style, with pinched rim and decorated with stylised bird and fish in bichrome black and red paint.

Amphora of the Cypro-Geometric White Painted ware, decorated with bands, parallel and zig-zag lines and solid black paint on rim, c. 950-850 BC.

The ancient city-kingdom of Soloi.

ARCHAIC AND
CLASSICAL PERIOD (750 - 310 BC)

Prosperity continued, but the island fell prey to several conquerors. Cypriot kingdoms were ruled by a succession of foreign cultures: after the Assyrians came the Egyptians and then the Persians. During the Archaic period we have evidence that in various areas of Cyprus local workshops and styles were developed. This period is characterised by the ability of Cypriot craftsmen not to imitate, but to produce something genuinely Cypriot.

King Evagoras of Salamis (who ruled from 411 - 374 BC) unified Cyprus and made the island one of the leading political and cultural centres of the Greek world. The culture of the Classical period was strongly influenced by Greek art and customs. King Evagoras invited many Greek artists and intellectuals to visit Cyprus and teach the Greek way of life and spirit.

The city-kingdoms of Cyprus welcomed Alexander the Great, King of Macedonia, and Cyprus became part of his empire. Alexander granted them autonomy, and this was the first time in many centuries that the city-kingdoms of Cyprus became autonomous. However, this situation did not last long.

Gold earring in the shape of a sitting sphinx, fourth-fifth century BC.

Some of the 2000 clay figurines found at the sanctuary at Agia Irini, in the Morfou area in northwest Cyprus, 750 - 500 BC.

22

Bronze cauldron supported on an iron tripod from the "Royal" Tomb 79 at Salamis, with decoration of eight griffin protomes and four double-faced sirens on its rim.

Wooden bed from the "Royal" Tomb 79 at Salamis, inlaid with ivory and dated to the end of the eighth century BC.

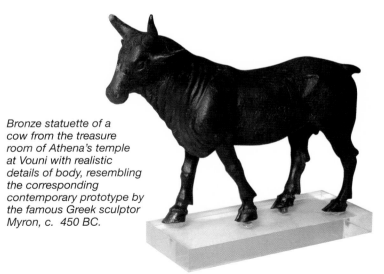

Bronze statuette of a cow from the treasure room of Athena's temple at Vouni with realistic details of body, resembling the corresponding contemporary prototype by the famous Greek sculptor Myron, c. 450 BC.

Silver coin minted at Kition, 180 - 145 BC.

HELLENISTIC PERIOD (310 - 30 BC)

After the rivalries for succession between Alexander's generals, Cyprus eventually came under the Hellenistic state of the Ptolemies of Egypt and from then on belonged to the Greek Alexandrine world. The Ptolemies abolished the city-kingdoms and unified Cyprus. Pafos became the capital.

Cultural life developed further. Theatres were built in major cities of the island and performances of comedies and tragedies were staged. Cypriot arts and crafts lost their originality and depended entirely on the Hellenistic style based on Greek models that had developed in the wider region of the Eastern Mediterranean.

Limestone head of a young woman from Arsos with symmetrical facial characteristics, recalling the corresponding works of the great Greek sculptor Myron, c. 300 BC.

Marble statue of Aphrodite from Soloi, whose arms and feet are missing. The rest facial characteristics and body details resemble similar statues from Cyrene, c.100 – 50 BC.

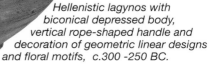

Hellenistic lagynos with biconical depressed body, vertical rope-shaped handle and decoration of geometric linear designs and floral motifs, c.300 -250 BC.

*Ancient Odeon in Pafos:
The Theatre is located
in the northeastern part
of the ancient city. The
construction of the theatre
dates to the founding of
the city (300 BC).*

*Limestone portrait of
Alexander the Great
from Soloi, 325-150 BC.*

ROMAN PERIOD (30 BC - 330 AD)

Cyprus came under the dominion of the Roman Empire. The most important event in the early years of Roman rule was the introduction of the Christian faith. During the missionary journey of Apostles Paul and Barnabas, the Proconsul Sergius Paulus was converted to Christianity, and Cyprus became the first country to be governed by a Christian.

Destructive earthquakes occurred during the first century BC and the first century AD and cities needed to be rebuilt. In 313 the Edict of Milan granted religious freedom in the Roman Empire, and Cypriot bishops attended the Council of Nicaea in 325.

During the Roman period, Cyprus was divided into four districts: Pafos, Salamis, Amathus and Lapithos. Many important public works were carried out. Theatres, gymnasia, and stadia were built in various parts of the island.

Cyprus under the Roman Empire preserved its Greek character. Most of the important mosaics discovered in Kourion and Pafos, belonging to the second century AD, confirm the continuation of Greek forms of religion and the worship of Greek deities on the island.

Floor mosaic from the House of Dionysos, Pafos, third century AD.

Floor mosaic representing Centaur and Maenad, Pafos, fourth century AD.

Leda and the Swan, floor mosaic from the Roman House of Leda, Pafos, late second or early third century AD.

26

The Bust of Ktisis, Curium Baths.

The ancient theatre of Kourion, 50-175 AD.

Over-lifesize bronze statue of the Roman Emperor Septimius Severus, 193-211 AD, found at the village of Kythrea, now in the Cyprus Museum.

27

BYZANTINE PERIOD (330 - 1191)

When the capital of the Roman Empire was transferred by the Constantine the Great to "New Rome" - Constantinople - and the foundations of the Byzantine Empire were laid in 330, Cyprus became part of Byzantium. Christianity became the official religion.

New earthquakes during the fourth century AD completely destroyed the cities of Salamis, Kition and Pafos. Once again, new cities arose. Constantia, built near the site of ancient Salamis, became the capital, and large basilicas were built during the fourth and fifth centuries.

During the Byzantine period Cyprus shared with the rest of the Hellenic world the same Christian and Greek culture and heritage.

The seventh century AD saw the rise and spread of Islam. The Arabs began their raids to Cyprus in 649. Although for three centuries Cyprus had been constantly under attack by Arabs, until 965, Arab presence and influence remained incidental and sporadic.

During the Byzantine period Cyprus shared with the rest of the Hellenic world the same Christian and Greek culture and heritage. Throughout this period a great number of monasteries and churches were built, many of which survive to this day. Some are decorated with unique frescoes and icons that have attracted worldwide attention and study.

The Monastery of Ayios Ioannis (St John) Lambadhistis, Kalopanayiotis, Troodos. It was built in the 11th century and decorated in the 11th and 13th centuries.

The Church of Ayios Nikolaos (St Nicholas) tis Steyis, Kakopetria, Troodos. It was built in the 11th century and completed in the 12th-13th centuries.

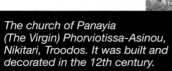

The church of Panayia (The Virgin) Phorviotissa-Asinou, Nikitari, Troodos. It was built and decorated in the 12th century.

The church of Panayia (The Virgin) tou Araka, Lagoudhera, Troodos. It was built and decorated in 1192.

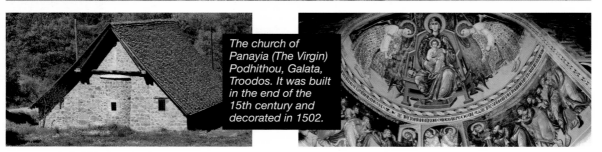

The church of Panayia (The Virgin) Podhithou, Galata, Troodos. It was built in the end of the 15th century and decorated in 1502.

31

history
richard the lionheart
and the knights templar
1191-1192

RICHARD THE LIONHEART AND THE KNIGHTS TEMPLAR (1191 - 1192)

Isaac Comnenus, a Byzantine governor and self-proclaimed emperor of Cyprus, behaved discourteously toward survivors of a shipwreck involving ships of King Richard's fleet on their way to the Holy Land during the Third Crusade. Among the survivors were Richard's sister Joanna, Queen of Sicily, and his betrothed Berengaria of Navarre. Richard in revenge fought Isaac, defeated him, took possession of Cyprus and married Berengaria of Navarre in Limassol, where she was crowned Queen of England.

A year later, Richard sold the island for 100.000 dinars to the Knights Templar, a Frankish military order, who resold it at the same price to Guy de Lusignan, deposed King of Jerusalem.

Richard the Lionheart comes ashore at Limassol.

Richard the Lionheart lands in Cyprus.

richard the lionheart
and the knights templar
1191-1192

*The Kolossi castle,
built by the Knights of
St John of Jerusalem
during the Crusades.*

FRANKISH (LUSIGNAN) PERIOD
(1192 - 1489)

Cyprus was ruled on the feudal system. The Catholic Church officially replaced the Greek Orthodox, which, though under severe suppression, managed to survive. The city of Famagusta (Ammochostos) was then one of the richest in the Near East. It was during this period that the historical names of Lefkosia, Ammochostos and Lemesos were changed to Nicosia, Famagusta and Limassol, respectively. The era of the Lusignan dynasty ended when Queen Catherine Cornaro ceded Cyprus to Venice in 1489.

Lusignan's Blazon.

During the Frankish period some magnificent Latin Cathedrals and castles were built. The Cathedral of St Sophia in Nicosia was built on the same design as that of Notre Dame of Paris. The Lusignan kings were crowned in this cathedral as kings of Cyprus. Another Gothic style Latin Cathedral, St Nicholas, was built in Famagusta, almost identical to the St Sophia Cathedral in Nicosia. At this Cathedral the Lusignan kings of Cyprus were crowned as kings of Jerusalem. Both Cathedrals were later converted into mosques by the Ottomans.

The Cathedral of Ayia Sophia turned into a mosque, in the occupied part of Nicosia.

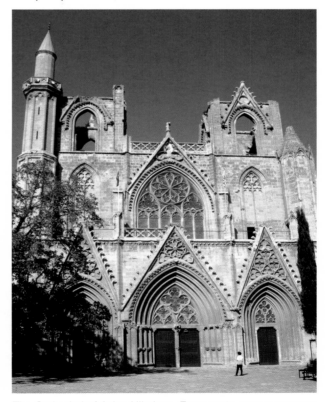

The Cathedral of Ayios Nikolaos, Famagusta, now a mosque.

The Gothic abbey at Pellapais, Kyrenia.

The St Hilarion castle on Pentadaktylos Range.

VENETIAN PERIOD (1489 - 1571)

The Venetians viewed Cyprus as the last bastion against the Ottomans in the Eastern Mediterranean and fortified the island, tearing down lovely buildings in Nicosia to reduce the boundaries of the city within fortified walls. They also built impressive walls around Famagusta which were considered at the time as state of the art military architecture.

Venetian Walls in Nicosia.

The Othello Tower and the Lion of Venice, Famagusta Walls.

The Famagusta Gate of the Nicosia Venetian Walls, with the interior rooms and the passage way used today as a cultural centre.

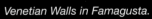

Venetian Walls in Famagusta.

OTTOMAN OCCUPATION (1571 - 1878)

Dragoman Hadjigeorgakis Kornesios, 1795.

In 1570 Ottoman troops attacked Cyprus, captured Nicosia, slaughtered twenty thousand of the population and laid siege on Famagusta for a year. After a brave defence by Venetian commander Marc Antonio Bragadin, Famagusta fell to Lala Mustafa Pasha, who at first allowed the besieged a peaceful exodus, but later ordered the flaying of Bragadin. On annexation to the Ottoman Empire, Lala Mustafa Pasha became the first governor. The Ottoman Turks were to rule Cyprus until 1878.

During the Ottoman period, the Muslim minority eventually acquired a Cypriot identity. Initially, the Greek Orthodox Church was granted a certain amount of autonomy, the feudal system was abolished and the freed serfs were allowed to acquire land. They were, however, heavily taxed. As the power of the Ottoman Turks declined, their rule became increasingly brutal and corrupt. In many instances Greek and Turkish Cypriots struggled together against the oppression of Ottoman rule. It was with a certain amount of optimism which proved to be sadly misplaced that Cyprus would be united with Greece that British rule was welcomed by the Greek Cypriots.

Ottoman baths, Nicosia.

The Bekir Pasha Aqueduct outside the city of Larnaka, built in 1746.

The siege of Nicosia by the Ottomans, 1570.

The Buyuk Han, Nicosia, was built in 1572 by the first Ottoman governor of Cyprus, Muzaffer Pasha.

BRITISH RULE (1878–1960)

As so often in the past, it was great power rivalry and strategic ambition that led to Cyprus changing hands yet again. Britain's main motive in acquiring the island in 1878 was to combat Russian influence in the Mediterranean and to protect its route to India. Britain was concerned about the Russian victory over the Ottomans in 1877, which increased Russian influence in the Eastern Mediterranean. Thus, at the Congress of Berlin the following year, where the British tried to weaken Russian influence, they signed a secret agreement with the Ottomans, whereby they would rent Cyprus from the Ottomans, in return for protecting the latter against Russia.

> Under the terms of the Treaty of Lausanne of 1923, the new Republic of Turkey ceded Cyprus to Britain and renounced all claims over territories under its former jurisdiction.

The British administration granted the local population a greater degree of autonomy than previously enjoyed, in the form of a legislative council consisting of Christian Orthodox, British officials and Moslems. The Moslems and British officials balanced the Christian Orthodox, with the casting vote going to the British High Commissioner.

In 1914, following the Ottoman Empire's entry into the First World War on the side of Germany, Britain annexed Cyprus, and then offered it to Greece, provided that the latter entered the war against Germany. By the time Greece joined in 1917, the offer had been withdrawn. Under the terms of the Treaty of Lausanne of 1923, the new Republic of Turkey ceded Cyprus to Britain and renounced all claims over territories under its former jurisdiction. In 1925, Britain declared Cyprus a Crown Colony.

Hoisting the British flag at Nicosia, the capital of Cyprus. (The illustrated London News, 10 August 1878).

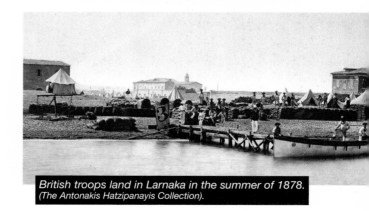

British troops land in Larnaka in the summer of 1878. (The Antonakis Hatzipanayis Collection).

The burning of the Government House during the "Octovriana" anticolonial uprising of 1931.

From the talks in London (Lancaster House) in February 1959 to finalise the Zurich-London Agreements that established the Republic of Cyprus.

41

THE LIBERATION MOVEMENT

Given the overwhelming majority of those of Greek stock and culture, combined with the power and pressure of the Church of Cyprus, a movement for liberation and union with Greece was as natural as it was inevitable, although the British Colonial Office tried to play down the question. Agitation came to the fore in 1931, when there was rioting, Government House was burnt down and the constitution was revoked, never to return.

> Britain's response to the liberation campaign was to work secretly with the Turkish Cypriots and the Turkish government, helping the latter to refine its propaganda.

During the Second World War, calls for union with Greece began again. When the Dodecanese were handed to Greece in 1947, these calls increased in strength, bolstered by the British pull-out from Palestine and impending pull-out from India.

In 1950, the Church of Cyprus organized a plebiscite among the Greek Christian Orthodox on enosis, with 96 percent voting in favor. The Greek government had been dealing with Britain bilaterally on the issue, but following British Foreign Minister Eden's, refusal to even discuss with Greece Cyprus' self-determination, matters began to come to a head, and the Greek government took the question to the UN General Assembly. In the meantime, the charismatic Archbishop Makarios III assumed the political leadership of the anti-colonial

Archbishop Makarios and Colonel Georgios Grivas-Digenis, the political and military leaders respectively, of the 1950s liberation struggle against British colonialism.

British colonial soldiers arrest Greek Cypriot civilians.

struggle. Colonel Georghios Grivas-Digenis launched and led a guerrilla campaign through the underground EOKA (National Organization of Cypriot Fighters) on 1 April 1955, to oust the British and achieve enosis.

Britain's response to the liberation campaign was to work secretly with the Turkish Cypriots and Turkey's government, helping the latter to refine its propaganda. As the struggle intensified, Britain decided that a useful way of keeping the issue out

EOKA freedom fighter Michalakis Karaolis is brought before a British colonial court (October 1955). He was executed by hanging (10 May 1956).

Archbishop Makarios
III upon his return to
Cyprus from British
imposed exile
(1 March 1959).

of the United Nations would be to hold a tripartite conference (Britain, Greece and Turkey). It was a way of again involving Turkey in Cyprus, in defiance of the Treaty of Lausanne. The conference broke down quickly, as the British government expected.

As the anti-colonial struggle to free Cyprus continued, Britain was working secretly with the Turkish authorities, encouraging them to demand partition. Turkey created the paramilitary Turkish Defense Organization (TMT) in the late 1950s to control the Turkish Cypriot community and their leadership, and to promote its partitionist policy on the island. The TMT stirred agitation against Greek Cypriots during the anti-colonial struggle and after independence. It was also responsible for the assassination of moderate Turkish Cypriots who opposed their partitionist designs.

The British discussed various proposals with Archbishop Makarios, one of them being the "Macmillan Plan." This would have entailed division of the island between Greek and Turkish Cypriots for seven years, followed by the joint sovereignty of Britain, Greece and Turkey. Only Turkey accepted the plan, which enabled Britain to continue the pressure. On 9 March 1956, for example, Britain deported Archbishop Makarios for over a

EOKA freedom fighters at the end of the 1955-59 anticolonial liberation struggle.

Memorial to EOKA freedom fighter Gregoris Afxentiou on the mountains of Machairas.

ΓΡΗΓΟΡΗΣ ΠΙΕΡΗ ΑΥΞΕΝΤΙΟΥ

year to the Seychelles. The United States, worried about the tension between NATO allies Greece and Turkey, increased its pressure on Britain, Greece and Turkey to find a way out of the impasse. Greek and Turkish Prime Ministers met in Zurich in February 1959.

They agreed on a draft plan for the independence of Cyprus under a Greek Cypriot and Turkish Cypriot president and vice-president respectively. On 19 February, in London, the Greek, Turkish and British governments met to finalise arrangements. The somewhat unique arrangements tended to detract from the idea of complete sovereignty and independence, in that the three treaties were clearly connected to a continuing British presence, and were considered as a single interconnected package by the British government.

The complexity of the whole postcolonial arrangement reflected a range of outside interests that detracted from the idea of a unitary state based on equal rights.

The "Imprisoned Tombs" at the Nicosia Central Prisons, where EOKA freedom fighters of the 1955-59 anticolonial struggle are buried.

Pupils demonstrating during the anti-colonial struggle.

Signing of the Treaty establishing the Republic of Cyprus (Nicosia, 16 August 1959).

the republic of
cyprus

- INDEPENDENCE
- THE 1974 INVASION BY TURKEY
- SEEKING A NEGOTIATED SOLUTION
- THE DESTRUCTION OF CULTURAL HERITAGE

the republic
of cyprus
independence

INDEPENDENCE

Cyprus was proclaimed an independent, sovereign republic on 16 August 1960. The independence of Cyprus was based on the 1959 Zurich and London Agreements negotiated by Greece, Turkey and the United Kingdom. These agreements included a Constitution and three treaties: the Treaty of Guarantee, the Treaty of Alliance, and the Treaty of Establishment. These agreements ended 82 years of British rule following many years of a national liberation movement.

Active opposition to colonial rule came from the Greek Cypriot community, whose majority at the time aspired to union of Cyprus with Greece. Turkey and the Turkish Cypriot leadership, on the other hand, prompted by the British, advocated partition of the island. These diametrically opposed visions were later specifically prohibited by the 1959 agreements that established Cyprus' independence. British rule did not encourage the emergence of a Cypriot national identity. Instead, Britain used the "divide and rule" policy as an instrument to control anticolonial sentiment on the island. It enlisted Turkish Cypriots on its side against the Greek Cypriot liberation movement, thereby planting the seeds of intercommunal discord and polarization between Greek and Turkish Cypriots, a development that was to prove detrimental to their cooperation upon independence.

Although they eventually signed the Zurich and London agreements, the Greek and Turkish Cypriot communities had no serious role in their drafting or in the drafting of the Constitution for the new republic. They were never given the opportunity to vote on

President Makarios with UN Secretary-General U Thant at UN headquarters in New York (26 October 1970).

them. In effect, they were imposed on the people of Cyprus.

Certain provisions of the agreements and the constitution, rather than promoting peace through intercommunal solidarity and loyalty to a common state as well as respect for the sovereignty of the new republic, proved conducive to domestic conflict and foreign interference. It soon became clear that Cyprus was granted a fettered independence and dysfunctional constitutional arrangements. The constitution itself emphasised differences between Greek and Turkish Cypriots, thereby thwarting integrative tendencies and encouraging divisive behaviour between the two communities.

The agreements provided for complex power sharing arrangements between the two communities (the Greek Cypriot numerical majority community of 82 percent of the population and the Turkish Cypriot numerical minority community of 18 percent of the

*Meeting of the first
Council of Ministers of
the newly established
Republic of Cyprus (1960).*

President Makarios and Vice President Fazil Kutchuck welcome Queen Elizabeth II at the Akrotiri British Sovereign Base Area (20 January 1961).

Turkish Cypriots from around the island, under pressure from their leadership, started concentrating into certain areas, in line with Turkey's policy to form Turkish enclaves under its control in order to separate the two communities as a first step toward the partition of Cyprus along ethnic lines.

President John F. Kennedy and President Makarios in Washington during a state visit by the Cypriot leader (5 June 1962).

population) and granted extraordinary veto powers to the Turkish Cypriot community. The three guarantor powers (Greece, Turkey, and the United Kingdom) were given vaguely defined rights to interfere in Cypriot affairs under certain conditions. In addition, the United Kingdom retained "sovereign base areas" that amount to 2.7 percent of the territory of the island as well as important intelligence gathering facilities, while Greece and Turkey were to station small military contingents (numbering 950 and 650 troops respectively) on the island.

The divisive nature of the constitution and the rigidity of its principal articles made the operation of a democratic government difficult and caused increasing acrimony between Greek and Turkish Cypriots. By 1963, a series of deadlocks over state budgets, taxation, municipalities, and other issues led to a constitutional crisis that threatened to paralyse the operation of the government and the state. The president felt compelled to propose on 30 November certain constitutional modifications for discussion to "remove obstacles to the smooth functioning and development of the state." The government of Turkey, however, rejected the suggested constitutional amendments. The Turkish Cypriot leadership followed suit and subsequently fell in line with Turkey's long-term policy to partition the island.

INTERCOMMUNAL CONFLICT

The atmosphere on Cyprus became tense and volatile. Relations between the two communities

President Makarios meets Egyptian leader Gamal Abdel Nasser and Yugoslav leader Josip Broz Tito, during the Non-Aligned Conference in Cairo (October 1964).

President Makarios with U.S. Secretary of State Henry Kissinger and Russian Minister of Foreign Affairs Andrei Gromyko in Nicosia, where the foreign dignitaries held talks on the Middle East (7 May 1974).

deteriorated as a series of events snowballed into a crisis extending beyond the borders of Cyprus. Isolated minor incidents escalated into intercommunal clashes. Turkish Cypriots from around the island, under pressure from their leadership, started concentrating into certain areas, in line with

President Makarios with leaders of the Non-Aligned Movement.

Turkey's policy to form Turkish enclaves under its control in order to separate the two communities as a first step toward the partition of Cyprus along ethnic lines. Eventually, Turkish Cypriots withdrew from all state institutions and government agencies. There were flare-ups of intercommunal violence in 1963–64 and again in 1967. International pressure prevented a military invasion by Turkey in 1964 and 1967.

Following the threats by Turkey, the government of the Republic brought the matter to the United Nations (UN). The Security Council unanimously adopted resolution 186 of 4 March 1964, whose basic principles have guided international actions on Cyprus ever since. This resolution:

President Makarios visits Ermou Street, after the outbreak of the intercommunal riots in Nicosia (December 1963).

> Following the threats by Turkey, the government of the Republic brought the matter to the United Nations (UN). The Security Council unanimously adopted resolution 186 of 4 March 1964, whose basic principles have guided international actions on Cyprus ever since.

- Established the UN Secretary-General's mission of good offices aiming at a peaceful solution on the basis of an agreed settlement in accordance with the UN Charter
- Created UNFICYP, the UN peacekeeping force on Cyprus
- Reaffirmed the sovereignty and continuing existence of the Republic of Cyprus
- Reaffirmed the continuity of the government of the Republic of Cyprus.

Despite calls by the Security Council to respect the sovereignty and territorial integrity of the Republic of Cyprus and to abstain from the threat or use of force against it, Turkey bombed Cypriot villages in 1964.

UNFICYP soldier nurses a child injured during the bombings of the Tylliria region by Turkey's air force (August 1964).

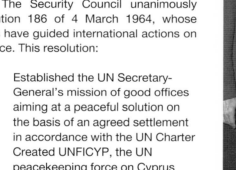

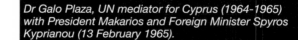

Dr Galo Plaza, UN mediator for Cyprus (1964-1965) with President Makarios and Foreign Minister Spyros Kyprianou (13 February 1965).

In 1965, UN mediator Dr Galo Plaza issued his report on Cyprus. Arguing strongly against the kind of settlement based on the geographical separation of the two communities that was advocated by the Turkish side, the report stated that:

The United Nations Peacekeeping Force in Cyprus (UNFICYP), created in 1964.

"if the purpose of a settlement of the Cyprus question is to be the preservation rather than the destruction of the state and if it is to foster rather than to militate against the development of a peacefully united people, I cannot help wondering whether the physical division of the minority from the majority should not be considered a desperate step in the wrong direction".

Turkey instantly rejected the report and its recommendations. UN mediation came to an end, and thereafter the UN involvement in the Cyprus peace process has been conducted under the Secretary-General's good offices.

The government of Cyprus took various measures to restore normalcy on the island resulting in the elimination of intercommunal violence and dramatic reduction of tensions between the two communities. The Turkish side did not reciprocate, maintaining, instead, roadblocks in order to keep Greek Cypriots from Turkish enclaves.

In 1968, the government initiated talks with the Turkish Cypriot leadership under UN auspices for a negotiated agreement to resolve outstanding constitutional issues. These promising talks were interrupted by the tragic events of 1974.

Commencement of UN sponsored intercommunal talks between Greek Cypriot Glafkos Clerides and Turkish Cypriot Rauf Denktash interlocutors in Nicosia (24 June 1968).

German Chancellor Willy Brandt with President Spyros Kyprianou at the 1974 UN ceasefire line in Nicosia (4 January 1982).

President Spyros Kyprianou with the Prime Minister of India Indira Gandhi in New Delhi (17 March 1983). Mrs Gandhi paid a visit to Cyprus in September 1983.

55

THE 1974 INVASION BY TURKEY

In 1967, a military junta seized power in Greece. The relationship between that regime and President Makarios of Cyprus became increasingly strained. Makarios was convinced that the junta was involved in efforts to undermine his authority and policies through extremist underground organizations in Cyprus.

President Makarios reviews the damage to the Presidential Palace as a result of the 1974 military coup by the junta of Greece.

On 15 July 1974, the junta and its Greek Cypriot collaborators carried out a coup against the democratically elected president of Cyprus. Using this criminal act as a pretext, and with Britain refusing to honour its obligations under the Treaty of Guarantee, Turkey invaded Cyprus five days later. In a two-phase invasion in July and August, and despite calls by the UN Security Council and the quick restoration of constitutional order on the island, Turkey occupied 36,2 percent of the sovereign territory of the Republic and forcibly expelled about 200.000 Greek Cypriots from their homes. Turkey still deprives the displaced Greek Cypriots of their right to return.

Turkey's occupation brought economic ruin to the part of the island which prior to 1974 was the richest and most developed.

In addition to the economic devastation caused by the invasion and the forcible population movement, over 3.000 persons were killed, while some 1.400 Greek Cypriots remain missing.

Turkey's occupation brought economic ruin to the part of the island which prior to 1974 was the richest and most developed. Poor economic conditions and Turkey's systematic colonization of the occupied

Turkey's invading forces on the shores of Kyrenia (20 July 1974).

areas with illegal settlers forced Turkish Cypriots to emigrate to Europe and elsewhere. The settlers currently outnumber the indigenous Turkish Cypriots by about two to one. There are still over 43.000 heavily armed troops from Turkey in the occupied

Greek Cypriot soldiers
captured by Turkey's
invading troops. They
were subsequently
executed.

Family members demand
ascertainment of the fate
of Cypriot missing persons
as a result of Turkey's
1974 invasion.

areas, even though, beginning with Security Council Resolution 353(1974), the UN has called for "an immediate end to foreign military intervention in the Republic of Cyprus," and for "the withdrawal without delay from the Republic of Cyprus of foreign military personnel present otherwise than under the authority of international agreements."

In addition, and in violation of international law, Turkey has systematically attempted to eradicate the Greek cultural heritage in the occupied areas. Towns and villages have been given Turkish names, while archaeological sites, churches and cemeteries have been plundered, damaged or converted to other uses.

A child at a Greek Cypriot refugee camp following Turkey's 1974 invasion of Cyprus.

For all legal and political purposes, the international community recognizes only the Republic of Cyprus created in 1960 and its government, even though the government cannot currently exercise its authority in areas under military occupation by Turkey.

In November 1983, Turkey instigated and endorsed a "unilateral declaration of independence" in the occupied area by the Turkish Cypriot leadership. The so-called "Turkish Republic of Northern Cyprus" ("TRNC") has not been recognized by anyone other than Turkey, which exercises virtual control over it. The UN Security Council categorically condemned this unilateral action, declared it invalid, called for its withdrawal, and called on all UN member-states not to recognise this illegal entity. The EU and other international and regional organizations have adopted similar positions. For all legal and political purposes, the international community recognises only the Republic of Cyprus created in 1960 and its government, even though the government cannot currently exercise its authority in areas under military occupation by Turkey.

Legal decisions by regional and national courts in Western Europe, in the United States, and in the

Illegal settlers from Turkey arriving in Kyrenia after the 1974 invasion of Cyprus by Turkey.

Return of Greek Cypriot prisoners of war captured by Turkey's invading troops (September 1974).

Greek Cypriot children receive food rations at a refugee camp following Turkey's 1974 invasion of Cyprus.

United Kingdom provide an important independent record of the consequences of Turkey's 1974 invasion and its continuing occupation of Cyprus. They also affirm the legitimacy of the Republic of Cyprus and of its government.

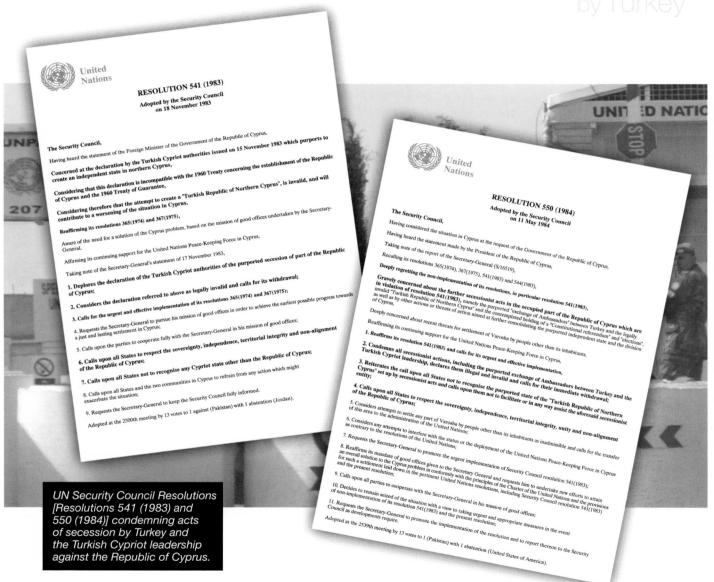

RESOLUTION 541 (1983)

Adopted by the Security Council on 18 November 1983

The Security Council,

Having heard the statement of the Foreign Minister of the Government of the Republic of Cyprus,

Concerned at the declaration by the Turkish Cypriot authorities issued on 15 November 1983 which purports to create an independent state in northern Cyprus,

Considering that this declaration is incompatible with the 1960 Treaty concerning the establishment of the Republic of Cyprus and the 1960 Treaty of Guarantee,

Considering therefore that the attempt to create a "Turkish Republic of Northern Cyprus", is invalid, and will contribute to a worsening of the situation in Cyprus,

Reaffirming its resolutions 365(1974) and 367(1975),

Aware of the need for a solution of the Cyprus problem, based on the mission of good offices undertaken by the Secretary-General,

Affirming its continuing support for the United Nations Peace-Keeping Force in Cyprus,

Taking note of the Secretary-General's statement of 17 November 1983,

1. **Deplores the declaration of the Turkish Cypriot authorities of the purported secession of part of the Republic of Cyprus;**

2. **Considers the declaration referred to above as legally invalid and calls for its withdrawal;**

3. **Calls for the urgent and effective implementation of its resolutions 365(1974) and 367(1975);**

4. Requests the Secretary-General to pursue his mission of good offices in order to achieve the earliest possible progress towards a just and lasting settlement in Cyprus;

5. Calls upon the parties to cooperate fully with the Secretary-General in his mission of good offices;

6. **Calls upon all States to respect the sovereignty, independence, territorial integrity and non-alignment of the Republic of Cyprus;**

7. **Calls upon all States not to recognise any Cypriot state other than the Republic of Cyprus;**

8. Calls upon all States and the two communities in Cyprus to refrain from any action which might exacerbate the situation;

9. Requests the Secretary-General to keep the Security Council fully informed.

Adopted at the 2500th meeting by 13 votes to 1 against (Pakistan) with 1 abstention (Jordan).

RESOLUTION 550 (1984)

Adopted by the Security Council on 11 May 1984

The Security Council,

Having considered the situation in Cyprus at the request of the Government of the Republic of Cyprus,

Having heard the statement made by the President of the Republic of Cyprus,

Taking note of the report of the Secretary-General (S/16519),

Recalling its resolutions 365(1974), 367(1975), 541(1983) and 544(1983),

Deeply regretting the non-implementation of its resolutions,

Gravely concerned about the further secessionist acts in the occupied part of the Republic of Cyprus which are in violation of resolution 541(1983), namely the purported "exchange of Ambassadors" between Turkey and the legally invalid "Turkish Republic of Northern Cyprus" and the contemplated holding of a "Constitutional referendum" and "elections", as well as by other actions or threats of action aimed at further consolidating the purported independent state and the division of Cyprus,

Deeply concerned about recent threats for settlement of Varosha by people other than its inhabitants,

Reaffirming its continuing support for the United Nations Peace-Keeping Force in Cyprus,

1. **Reaffirms its resolution 541(1983) and calls for its urgent and effective implementation,**

2. **Condemns all secessionist actions, including the purported exchange of Ambassadors between Turkey and the Turkish Cypriot leadership, declares them illegal and invalid and calls upon their immediate withdrawal,**

3. **Reiterates the call upon all States not to recognise the purported state of the "Turkish Republic of Northern Cyprus" set up by secessionist acts and calls upon them not to facilitate or in any way assist the aforesaid secessionist entity;**

4. **Calls upon all States to respect the sovereignty, independence, territorial integrity, unity and non-alignment of the Republic of Cyprus;**

5. Considers attempts to settle any part of Varosha by people other than its inhabitants as inadmissible and calls for the transfer of this area to the administration of the United Nations;

6. Considers any attempts to interfere with the status or the deployment of the United Nations Peace-Keeping Force in Cyprus as contrary to the resolutions of the United Nations;

7. Requests the Secretary-General to promote the urgent implementation of Security Council resolution 541(1983);

8. Reaffirms its mandate of good offices given to the Secretary General and requests him to undertake new efforts to attain an overall solution to the Cyprus problem in conformity with the principles of the Charter of the United Nations and the provisions for such a settlement laid down in the pertinent United Nations resolutions, including Security Council resolution 541(1983) and the present resolution;

9. Calls upon all parties to cooperate with the Secretary-General in his mission of good offices;

10. Decides to remain seized of the situation with a view to taking urgent and appropriate measures in the event of non-implementation of its resolution 541(1983) and the present resolution;

11. Requests the Secretary-General to promote the implementation of the resolution and to report thereon to the Security Council as developments require.

Adopted at the 2539th meeting by 13 votes to 1 (Pakistan) with 1 abstention (United States of America).

UN Security Council Resolutions [Resolutions 541 (1983) and 550 (1984)] condemning acts of secession by Turkey and the Turkish Cypriot leadership against the Republic of Cyprus.

59

Meeting of President Makarios with Turkish Cypriot leader Rauf Denktash under the auspices of UN Secretary-General Kurt Waldheim (12 February 1977).

In 1975, the UN Security Council reactivated the Secretary-General's mission of good offices, which had been interrupted in 1974.

Meeting of President Spyros Kyprianou with Turkish Cypriot leader Rauf Denktash in the presence of UN Secretary-General Perez de Cuellar (19 May 1979).

SEEKING A NEGOTIATED SOLUTION

The Cyprus problem has since 1974 been one of military invasion and continuing occupation in violation of relevant unanimous UN Security Council resolutions. Negotiations, especially after 2002, aimed at a comprehensive solution for the reunification of Cyprus. Throughout this process, the government of Cyprus sought a solution reflecting democratic norms, the UN Security Council resolutions, international law, European Union law, and relevant court decisions. The Turkish side, on the other hand, demanded a solution that would keep the two communities apart, either as two separate sovereign states or two separate states under a loose confederation.

The two communities agreed in 1977 and 1979 to reunite Cyprus under a federal republic. For the Greek Cypriots, who had strongly advocated the concept of a unitary state, the acceptance of a federation was the ultimate concession and historic compromise in their effort to terminate Turkey's occupation and achieve the reunification of Cyprus.

The UN-led peace process has since 1977 sought to define the framework of such a federal solution. Negotiations have sought to reconcile the interests and concerns of the two sides under a common central government. Issues of definitions of objectives and ways to implement a comprehensive federal settlement became serious problems mainly because of the intransigence of Turkey.

In 1975, the UN Security Council reactivated the Secretary-General's mission of good offices, which had been interrupted in 1974. Since then, intermittent negotiations under UN auspices have taken place, but failed for a number of reasons, including:

- Failure to implement UN Security Council resolutions
- Prevalence of third-party strategic considerations over a viable and functional solution that satisfies the concerns of the state of Cyprus and of all Cypriots
- Intransigent policies of successive governments in Turkey
- Disregard of international law and European law.

The UN process, having gone through various stages, culminated in the UN proposal known as the "Annan Plan," which was submitted to the parties first in November 2002 and subsequently, in its final form ("Annan V"), in March 2004.

President George Vassiliou with UN Secretary-General Boutros Boutros-Ghali (April 1992).

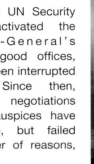

President Glafkos Clerides meets with UN Secretary-General Kofi Annan at UN headquarters (21 December 1999).

ΚΑΛΩΣ ΗΛΘΑΤΕ

Greek Prime Minister
Andreas Papandreou
with President Spyros
Kyprianou during his
official visit to Cyprus
(27 February 1982).

61

UN NEGOTIATIONS, 2002–2004

This period marks the more sustained effort of the UN for a comprehensive settlement of the Cyprus problem. Earlier efforts foundered over the Turkish demand for recognition of the illegal "state" in the areas of the Republic occupied by Turkey.

In an attempt to secure an agreement by the December 2002 Copenhagen EU summit, which would decide on the accession of Cyprus to the EU in 2004, Secretary-General Kofi Annan presented on 11 November 2002 a detailed plan for a comprehensive settlement (Annan I). The plan was revised on 10 December 2002 (Annan II) and again on 26 February 2003 (Annan III).

> The Secretary-General met with the leaders of the two communities at the Hague in March 2003 to ascertain whether they were prepared to submit Annan III to referenda. The Turkish side rejected the UN proposal.

The Secretary-General met with the leaders of the two communities at the Hague in March 2003 to ascertain whether they were prepared to submit Annan III to referenda. The Turkish side rejected the UN proposal.

In early 2003, massive Turkish Cypriot demonstrations took place in the occupied areas against the Turkish Cypriot leader and his Ankara supported policies.

Usurpation of Greek Cypriot properties in the Turkish occupied areas.

UN Secretary-General Kofi Annan with President Tassos Papadopoulos, former President Glafkos Clerides and Turkish Cypriot leader Rauf Denktas during his visit to Cyprus (28 February 2003).

Cyprus, as expected, signed the EU Treaty of Accession on 16 April 2003.

On 23 April 2003, under growing public Turkish Cypriot discontent with the situation in occupied Cyprus, Turkey and the Turkish Cypriot leadership were compelled to partially lift restrictions, which they had imposed since 1974 along the UN ceasefire line, on the movement of Greek and Turkish Cypriots. Since then, thousands of Cypriots have been crossing regularly the ceasefire line. These peaceful crossings have destroyed the myth cultivated for years by Turkish propaganda that the two communities cannot live together.

On the consensus that emerged in meetings with Turkey's prime minister in Washington, in January 2004, the U.S. administration persuaded the UN Secretary-General to call for a resumption of negotiations in New York.

On 13 February 2004, it was agreed by the parties that negotiations would commence for changes that

*From the meeting
in Bürgenstock,
Switzerland under
the auspices of UN
Secretary-General Kofi
Annan (31 March 2004).*

fell within the parameters of Annan III. In case of continuing deadlock, the Secretary-General would finalize a text which would then be submitted to the two communities on Cyprus for a vote.

This was a significant change in the UN Secretary-General's mission of good offices as had been conceived since 1964. Without Security Council authorisation, the Secretary-General assumed the power of arbitrator as a precondition for the new round of talks. By the time of the talks in Switzerland late in March 2004, the Secretariat became a partial party to the dispute by promoting most of Turkey's positions on the Cyprus problem.

The change in the Secretary-General's role, coupled with extremely tight negotiating deadlines and Turkey's intransigence, contributed to the absence of serious negotiations. In order to gain Turkey's consent, nearly all of its demands were incorporated arbitrarily in the two plans (Annan IV and V), presented by the Secretary-General. Annan V was presented to the two sides on 31 March 2004. Turkey, the United States and the United Nations agreed to accept the EU presence only on an observer status in the talks, while the EU made the commitment to accommodate the derogations from European law that were included in Annan V. The Secretary-General's plan, a complex legal document of nearly 10.000 pages, was not available in its totality on the UN website until hours before the referendum. Cypriots were called to vote on the document on 24 April 2004, only days before the accession of the Republic of Cyprus to the EU on 1 May.

THE PEOPLE'S DECISION

Following a spirited public debate, Greek Cypriot voters overwhelmingly rejected Annan V, by a vote of 75,8 percent against 24,2 percent. In contrast, 64,9 percent of the Turkish Cypriot voters approved the plan. It should be noted that settlers from Turkey, who had no legal right to vote, were allowed to do so.

The Greek Cypriot "no" vote was not a vote against reunification or reconciliation. It was a rejection of a process that led to a one-sided plan perceived harmful to the legitimate rights of the Greek Cypriot community and to the survival of the state of Cyprus itself. It was a rejection of a flawed plan that did not provide for the genuine reunification of Cyprus, its institutions, people, and economy.

Ultimately, the plan was rejected because it was judged by the great majority of Cypriots not to be in the best common interest of Greek Cypriots and Turkish Cypriots. The negative outcome of the referendum rendered the Annan Plan null and void.

> Ultimately, the plan was rejected because it was judged by the great majority of Cypriots not to be in the best common interest of Greek Cypriots and Turkish Cypriots. The negative outcome of the referendum rendered the Annan Plan null and void.

REVIVING THE PEACE PROCESS 2005–2006

In order to revive the peace process, President Tassos Papadopoulos exchanged views with the Secretary-General in 2005 concerning the preparation of a renewed effort on Cyprus by the UN. The Secretary-General also met with Turkish Cypriot leader Mehmet Ali Talat. President Papadopoulos subsequently met with the Secretary-General in 2006 and examined modalities for moving forward on the peace process.

President Tassos Papadopoulos and Turkish Cypriot leader Mehmet Ali Talat meet in the presence of the UN Secretary-General's Special Representative in Cyprus, Ibrahim Gambari (8 July 2006).

THE 8 JULY 2006 AGREEMENT

This new momentum for the resumption of the peace process on Cyprus led to a "Set of Principles" (the 8 July 2006 Agreement) between the two communities. Among its provisions was a "commitment to the unification of Cyprus based on a bi-zonal, bicommunal federation and political equality, as set out in the relevant Security Council resolutions."

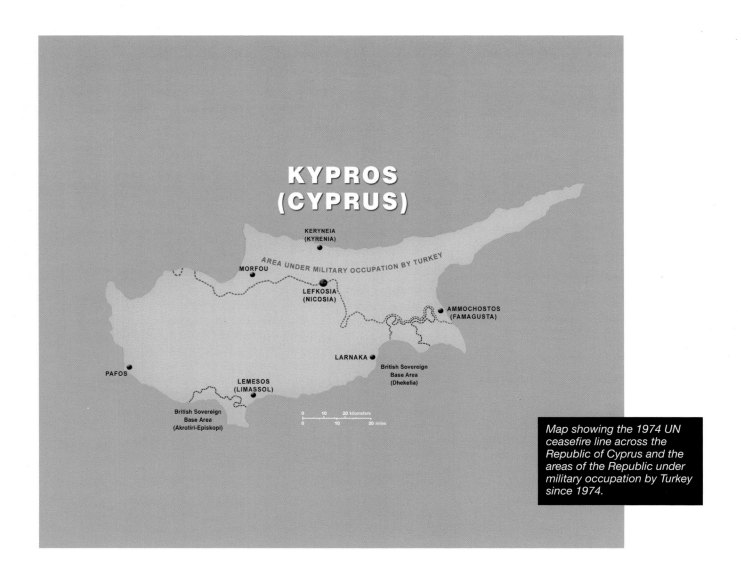

KYPROS
(CYPRUS)

KERYNEIA
(KYRENIA)

AREA UNDER MILITARY OCCUPATION BY TURKEY

MORFOU

LEFKOSIA
(NICOSIA)

AMMOCHOSTOS
(FAMAGUSTA)

LARNAKA

British Sovereign
Base Area
(Dhekelia)

PAFOS

LEMESOS
(LIMASSOL)

British Sovereign
Base Area
(Akrotiri-Episkopi)

0   10   20 kilometers
0   10   20 miles

Map showing the 1974 UN ceasefire line across the Republic of Cyprus and the areas of the Republic under military occupation by Turkey since 1974.

65

the republic
of cyprus
seeking a negotiated
solution

President Demetris Christofias and Turkish Cypriot leader Mehmet Ali Talat begin full-fledged negotiations in the presence of Alexander Downer, the UN Secretary-General's Special Advisor on Cyprus (3 September 2008).

NEW INITIATIVES IN 2008

Despite the setback caused by the Turkish refusal to implement the 8 July Agreement, the newly elected president of Cyprus, Demetris Christofias, sought, immediately after his inauguration on 28 February 2008, to meet with the Turkish Cypriot leader, in yet another effort to set in motion a process. He also embarked on a campaign to reenergize the international community toward a new peace process, in which the two communities would have the leading roles. These initiatives yielded positive results and gained support from the international community.

> President Christofias and Turkish Cypriot leader Talat started full-fledged negotiations on 3 September 2008, under the good offices mission of the United Nations Secretary-General. The talks continue with Mr Talat's successor Mr Dervish Eroglu.

FULL-FLEDGED DIRECT NEGOTIATIONS

President Christofias and Turkish Cypriot leader Talat started full-fledged negotiations on 3 September 2008, under the good offices mission of the United Nations Secretary-General. The talks continued with Mr Talat's successor Mr Dervish Eroglu.

Some concerns were raised because of comments made by the Turkish side at the start of the talks, which reiterated intransigent Turkish positions, such as insistence on maintaining guarantees and intervention rights by Turkey on Cyprus. Such attitude as well as subsequent hard-line statements by Turkey's leaders, cast a shadow on the negotiations. They run contrary to the positive, constructive, cooperative, and conciliatory spirit brought to this new effort by the Greek Cypriot side, which spirit is required for the success of the peace process.

Meanwhile, in order to emphasise the significance attributed by the UN to the peace negotiations, the UN Secretary-General paid a three-day visit

President Demetris Christofias and Turkish Cypriot leader Dervish Eroglu during intercommunal talks (2010).

to Cyprus in early 2010 to express his personal support for the talks. A statement was read out by the Secretary-General on behalf of the leaders of the two communities stressing that they have worked on the basis of the integrated whole approach that is "nothing is agreed until everything is agreed".

CONCLUSION

Having successfully joined the EU, the people of Cyprus still yearn for the reunification of their country. The government of Cyprus is determined to continue its search for a viable and functional solution within the parameters of the UN resolutions as well as the new political context created by the accession of Cyprus to the EU, in order to safeguard the rights of all Cypriots. In this manner, all Cypriots will fully enjoy the benefits and advantages of EU membership and bring about the reunification of their country after more than three decades of artificial division.

Initiatives by the government of Cyprus broke the deadlock, moved the peace process forward, and resulted in the commencement of full-fledged negotiations between the two communities. This development, directed toward a comprehensive settlement, has also reinvigorated the interest of the international community resulting in broad support for a viable settlement and permanent peace on Cyprus.

President Demetris Christofias with UN Secretary General Ban ki-moon at the UN headquarters in New York (21 September 2010).

THE DESTRUCTION
OF CULTURAL HERITAGE

"Damage to cultural property belonging to any people whatsoever means damage to the cultural heritage of all mankind." **Preamble of the 1954 Hague Convention for the Protection of Cultural Property in the Event of Armed Conflict**

The systematic and deliberate destruction and obliteration of the Greek Cypriot cultural heritage is the final touch in Turkey's policy of ethnic cleansing and of the colonization of occupied Cyprus.

Cyprus has been at the crossroads of civilisation in the Eastern Mediterranean. Its recorded history of more than 11,000 years is considered to be of central importance in the history of European art and civilisation. The systematic and deliberate destruction and obliteration of the Greek Cypriot cultural heritage is the final touch in Turkey's policy of ethnic cleansing and of the colonisation of occupied Cyprus. It is a tragic and irreversible consequence of the 1974 Turkish invasion. Turkey is in violation of international law and of major international conventions it signed and ratified, including the 1954 UNESCO Convention on the Protection of Cultural Property in the Event of Armed Conflict, the 1949 Fourth Geneva Convention, and the 1970 UNESCO Convention on the Illicit Import, Export and Transfer of Ownership of Cultural Property. The destruction of the Greek Cypriot cultural heritage has been enhanced by:

- The lure of money in the black market for art objects
- The unwillingness of the occupation authorities to devote the necessary resources to protect the Greek Cypriot cultural heritage
- The unwillingness of the occupation authorities to cooperate with UNESCO
- The attempt by the Turkish Cypriot subordinate local administration in occupied Cyprus to gain de facto recognition in return for its cooperation with international institutions
- The expulsion of foreign archaeological schools working in the northern part of Cyprus until the time of the Turkish invasion.

The crucifix from the Church of St Prokopios, Syngrassi, Famagusta district.

The Rizokarpaso Cemetery, the Karpass area.

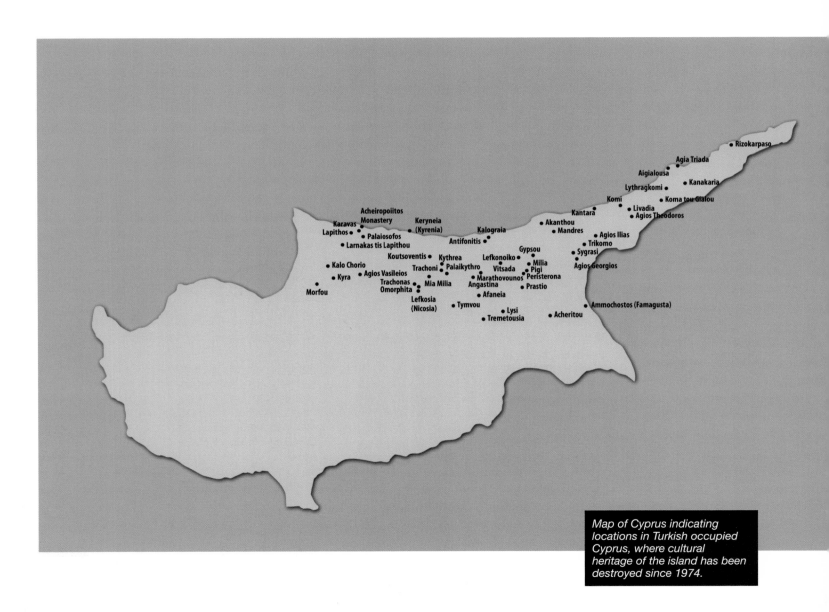

the destruction of cultural heritage

Rizokarpaso
Agia Triada
Aigialousa
Lythragkomi • Kanakaria
Komi • Koma tou Gialou
Kantara • Livadia
Akanthou • Agios Theodoros
Mandres
Agios Ilias
Trikomo
Sygrasi
Agios Georgios

Acheiropoiitos Monastery
Karavas
Keryneia (Kyrenia)
Lapithos •
Palaiosofos
Kalograia
Antifonitis
Larnakas tis Lapithou
Gypsou
Koutsoventis • Kythrea
Lefkonoiko
Kalo Chorio
Trachoni Palaikythro
Milia
Kyra Agios Vasileios
Vitsada
Pigi
Peristerona
Marathovounos
Trachonas Mia Milia
Angastina
Prastio
Morfou Omorphita
Afaneia
Lefkosia (Nicosia)
Tymvou
Lysi
Ammochostos (Famagusta)
Tremetousia
Acheritou

Map of Cyprus indicating locations in Turkish occupied Cyprus, where cultural heritage of the island has been destroyed since 1974.

Destruction of a wall-painting in the Antifonitis Monastery, Kyrenia district.

The deliberate destruction of the cultural heritage includes, but is not limited to:

- The destruction of ancient historic sites and monuments
- The looting of museums and other private collections
- The destruction and desecration of important religious sites to Orthodox, Maronite and Armenian Cypriots. Known as the "island of the saints", Cyprus has played an important role in the evolution and spread of Christianity in the West
- The deliberate name changes of historic sites, towns and villages in an attempt to erase the documented historic past of the island
- The destruction and disappearance of historical ancient artifacts and important movable religious items such as icons, sacerdotal vestments, books and precious items used in religious services
- The removal and illicit sale of historic frescoes and mosaics from UNESCO designated and protected religious sites, some dating back to the 6th century AD. Classic cases became those of the Antiphonitis frescoes and the Kanakaria mosaics whose recovery showed the depth of the official illicit networks and money involved in the black market for art objects. The removal of frescoes and mosaics requires scientific expertise, connivance and involvement of local authorities.

The historic wealth of occupied Cyprus is shown by the presence of:

- 31 major archaeological sites and ancient cemeteries
- 11 major fortresses, towers and fortifications
- 37 historic designated homes and bridges
- 520 churches, monasteries and chapels.

The fate of the churches and monasteries (Orthodox, Maronite and Armenian) is indicative of the systematic and deliberate policies of the occupation regime:

- 125 churches have been turned into mosques, an old Islamic tradition in occupied territories
- 67 have been turned into stables or hay warehouses
- 57 have become museums, cultural centers or hotels
- 17 have become hostels, restaurants or military warehouses
- 25 have been demolished
- 229 have been totally desecrated.

THE OFFICIAL RESPONSE

In an attempt to limit the damage to the Cypriot cultural heritage the government of Cyprus along with the Church of Cyprus have expanded their cooperation with foreign museums and auction houses to identify and seek the return of stolen historical and religious artifacts. In cooperation with Cypriot foundations they have also invested in the recovery of such items from the international market.

Occasionally, compromises have been made in which items of secondary importance were sacrificed for

In an attempt to limit the damage to the Cypriot cultural heritage the government of Cyprus along with the Church of Cyprus have expanded their cooperation with foreign museums and auction houses to identify and seek the return of stolen historical and religious artifacts.

*Destruction of the
wall-paintings
in the Antifonitis Monastery
in the Kyrenia district.*

71

The Kontea Cemetery, Famagusta district.

the recovery of more important historic artifacts and religious items. In addition, agreements have been reached for the temporary safekeeping of such items abroad, as in the case of the Menil Foundation of Houston.

Part of the costly and lengthy recovery process involves the requirements of foreign courts for proof of ownership. This is often difficult given the lack of access to records and facilities in occupied Cyprus and reliance on photographic evidence to identify stolen items.

The Church of Cyprus has also resorted to foreign courts to recover looted religious items. The case of the Kanakaria mosaics in the United States District Court in Indianapolis is one such example. The case involved the ownership of plundered sixth century Byzantine mosaics from the Church of Kanakaria in the occupied part of Cyprus. The mosaics had been removed by Turkish antiquities smugglers and sold to an American art dealer for $1.2 million. In a far ranging precedent setting decision on the protection of cultural property the Court, on 3 August 1989, ordered the return of the plundered mosaics to their legitimate owner, the Church of Cyprus. This decision was affirmed by the United States Court of Appeals for the Seventh Circuit on 24 October 1990.

> The government of Cyprus has also concluded bilateral agreements with foreign governments intended to protect its archaeological and cultural heritage.

The Marathovounos Cemetery, Famagusta district.

The government of Cyprus has also concluded bilateral agreements with foreign governments intended to protect its archaeological and cultural heritage. One such recent example is the

The church of Ayios Prokopios, Synkrasi, Famagusta district.

Memorandum of Understanding "To Protect the Archaeological and Ethnological Heritage of Cyprus" signed between the United States and the Republic of Cyprus in 2002 and extended for another five years in 2007.

The unending battle to protect the Cypriot cultural heritage and Turkey's unwillingness to cooperate with UNESCO and other international institutions to protect the Cypriot cultural heritage is one more example of Turkey's deliberate policy of eradicating the historic Greek Cypriot presence from occupied Cyprus.

The church of Panagia Chryseleousa, Kyrenia district.

The Sourp Magar (Saint Makarios) Armenian Monastery, Pentadactylos range.

"...Points out that the cultural heritage of each people must be preserved and condemns the systematic policy of expunging the past and the Hellenic and Christian culture pursued by Turkey in the part of Cyprus occupied by its troops, as regards both the imposition of place names and the disappearance or transformation of the island's cultural heritage..."
European Parliament Resolution, 10 March 1988.

CONCLUSION

The information that is available from independent sources leaves no doubt about Turkey's systematic and deliberate policy of eradicating all aspects of the Greek Cypriot heritage and presence in the occupied areas. These discriminatory policies were directed at Greek, Maronite and Armenian Cypriots because of their ethnicity, religion and language. This is a stigma on the international community at a time when, with support from the Republic of Cyprus, Turkey is engaged in accession talks with the EU. Turkey continues to violate its international obligations capitalising on regional instability and the support extended to Turkey by influential external powers. The subordination of human rights, including the protection of cultural heritage, to economic, political and security considerations undermines not only the European human rights regime, but also the European commitment to the rule of law, democracy and human rights. Cyprus, since 1974, was and remains the testing ground of these principles.

The subordination of human rights, including the protection of cultural heritage, to economic, political and security considerations undermines not only the European human rights regime, but also the European commitment to the rule of law, democracy and human rights.

The church of St George, Gastria, Famagusta district.

Destroyed mosaic of God Eurotas, Salamina.

"The political-demographic de facto partition imposed on Cyprus since 1974 thus threatens not only the unity and integrity of a modern nation-state but also the millennial cultural integrity and continuity of the island which has been the crossroads of the civilization of the eastern Mediterranean."
Michael Jansen, "Cyprus: The Loss of a Cultural Heritage," Modern Greek Studies Yearbook, University of Minnesota (1986).

The vandalised archaeological site of Soloi, Morfou area.

The vandalised Jewish Margo Cemetery, south-east of Nicosia.

Destruction of royal tombs in the ancient city of Salamina.

75

President George Vassiliou with King Juan Carlos and Queen Sofia of Spain in Madrid (25 October 1992).

President Glafkos Clerides meets with USA President Bill Clinton at the White House (24 June 1996).

President Tassos Papadopoulos with the President of the People's Republic of China Hu Jintao during his official visit to China (6 December 2006).

President Demetris Christofias meets with Russian President Dmitry Medvedev during his official visit to Russia (19 November 2008).

cyprus
in the world

- MEMBER OF THE UNITED NATIONS
- THE COUNCIL OF EUROPE
- THE ORGANISATION FOR SECURITY AND COOPERATION IN EUROPE
- THE COMMONWEALTH OF NATIONS
- THE EURO-MEDITERRANEAN PARTNERSHIP
- THE PATH TO EU MEMBERSHIP
- MEMBER OF THE EUROPEAN UNION

cyprus
in the world
member
of the united nations

MEMBER OF THE UNITED NATIONS

Soon after independence in 1960 the Republic of Cyprus became a member of the United Nations, the Commonwealth, the Non-Aligned Movement and the Council of Europe. Cyprus subsequently became a member of other international organisations, including the Organisation for Security and Cooperation in Europe, and the World Bank.

Cyprus has been a member of the United Nations since 20 September 1960. Cyprus firmly believes in the primacy of the United Nations and its Charter and contributes to the promotion of the purposes and principles of the United Nations.

The Security Council, the General Assembly and other bodies of the United Nations, including the Commission on Human Rights, the Sub-Commission on Prevention of Discrimination and Protection of Minorities, the Committee on the Elimination of Racial Discrimination and UNESCO, have been involved in the question of Cyprus and have adopted numerous resolutions on all aspects of the problem over the years.

Cyprus has been an active member of the United Nations and has been elected periodically to numerous committees and bodies of the Organisation. Cyprus is also a member of the United Nations specialized agencies and other autonomous bodies including the Food and Agricultural Organisation (FAO), the International Labour Organisation (ILO), the International Monetary Fund (IMF), the UN Education, Scientific and Culture Organisation (UNESCO), the World Health Union (WHO) , the World Trade Organisation (WTO) and others.

The United Nations headquarters in New York.

Pope Benedict XVI with President Demetris Christofias during his official visit to Cyprus (4-6 June 2010).

UN Security Council considers reports on Cyprus
by the UN Secretary-General (15 June 2010).

cyprus
in the world
the council of europe

President Demetris Christofias with the President of France Nicolas Sarkozy, in Paris. (2 September 2009).

THE COUNCIL OF EUROPE

Cyprus has been a member of the Council of Europe since May 1961 and participates in all its bodies and organs, including the Parliamentary Assembly.

Cyprus has always contributed actively to the implementation of the Council's principles and values, particularly in the field of safeguarding and promoting of human and social rights. Cypriot experts participate in most of the Council's specialized Committees and their contribution has been widely acknowledged.

Cyprus has assumed the Presidency of the Committee of Ministers of the Council of Europe, the top executive body of the Council, four times since its accession to the organisation.

The Council, responding to Cyprus' applications, has found Turkey, through reports of the European Commission of Human Rights and Decisions of the European Court of Human Rights, responsible for serious violations of the European Convention on Human Rights in the part of Cyprus occupied by Turkey.

The President of the House of Representatives, Marios Garoyian, addresses the European Conference of the Presidents of Parliaments held in Cyprus on 11 and 12 June 2010.

THE ORGANISATION FOR SECURITY AND COOPERATION IN EUROPE (OSCE)

Cyprus is one of the 35 signatory states of the Final Act concluded in Helsinki in 1975, and an active participant in the procedures of the then Conference for Security and Cooperation in Europe (CSCE), which on 1 January 1995 became an international organisation under the name Organisation for Security and Cooperation in Europe (OSCE). Since the conception of the CSCE in the early 1970s, Cyprus, together with the other neutral and non-aligned (N+N) states of Europe, have strived to make the CSCE a process of common European progress, where the division between East and West would gradually diminish and eventually disappear. Cyprus was a founding member of the group of the N+N countries, which assumed the role of bridge-building between the opposing interests of East and West.

The CSCE Conference in Vienna, which took place from November 1986 to January 1989, and its Concluding Document marked the new era in European relations following the rapprochement between East and West. Cyprus has made its contribution to the achievement of the results of the Vienna Conference promoting the finding of solutions to important issues such as the military security in Europe, the Mediterranean, the environment and the principles guiding relations between states.

In the field of the ten principles guiding the relations between states, known as the Helsinki Decalogue, Cyprus has promoted the adoption of new and concrete obligations concerning the territorial integrity of states and human rights. In particular, the adoption in the Vienna Concluding Document of provisions for the non-recognition of situations, which violate the territorial integrity of a state and the recognition of the right of all refugees to return to their homes in safety, underlines the influence of the Cypriot position.

Official visit by the President of the Hellenic Republic Karolos Papoulias to Cyprus (12 October 2005).

Greek Prime Minister George Papandreou during his official visit to Cyprus (19 October 2009).

THE COMMONWEALTH OF NATIONS

Cyprus became a member of the Commonwealth in 1961, soon after attaining its independence and has been participating actively in all Commonwealth activities. Cyprus hosted the Commonwealth Heads of Government Meeting in 1993.

The Commonwealth has consistently supported Cyprus in its struggle for a just and viable solution to the Cyprus problem. As an expression of their continued solidarity with the government and the people of Cyprus, the Heads of Government of Commonwealth countries at their Meeting in New Delhi, in 1983, agreed to establish a special Commonwealth Action Group on Cyprus to assist towards compliance with UN Security Council Resolution 541.

> The Commonwealth Heads of Government Meeting repeatedly expressed support for the independence, sovereignty, territorial integrity and unity of the Republic of Cyprus.

The resolution declared the 1983 secessionist act by the Turkish Cypriot leadership in occupied Cyprus as "legally invalid" and called for its withdrawal.

The Commonwealth Heads of Government Meeting repeatedly expressed support for the independence, sovereignty, territorial integrity and unity of the Republic of Cyprus. They have also repeatedly called for the implementation of all United Nations resolutions on Cyprus.

Apart from support given to Cyprus in its efforts to find a just and viable solution, Cyprus also receives technical and other assistance from the Commonwealth in the form of expert advice or in the field of education. On its part, the Republic of Cyprus offers scholarships to students from Commonwealth countries either directly or through the Commonwealth Fund for Technical Cooperation.

President Glafkos Clerides addresses the Commowealth Summit held in Cyprus (25 October 1993).

THE EURO-MEDITERRANEAN PARTNERSHIP

The Euro-Mediterranean Partnership provides the institutional structure for the development of relations between the European Union and the Mediterranean states. The Partnership was initiated with the Conference of EU and Mediterranean Foreign Ministers in Barcelona, on 27 and 28 November 1995. This event noted the start of a new "partnership" phase in the relationship including bilateral and multilateral or regional cooperation. Cyprus has participated in the Barcelona Process since its inauguration: as a Mediterranean Partner, together with Algeria, Egypt, Israel, Jordan, Lebanon, Malta, Morocco, the Palestinian Authority, Syria, Tunisia and Turkey, and as of the 1 May 2004, as a member of the Union in a Euro-Mediterranean Partnership that numbers 35 participating states.

Cyprus fully supports from the outset the Union for the Mediterranean and actively participates in the relevant deliberations, so that this new body succeeds in fulfilling the high tasks assigned to it.

The Republic of Cyprus, as a participant in the Barcelona Process since its creation, has followed the evolution of the Euro-Mediterranean Partnership very closely. As a Mediterranean country and a European Union member state, Cyprus is one of the more fervent supporters of the enhancement of the Mediterranean dimension of the Union's foreign policy.

Furthermore, as a country with historical, cultural, and commercial bonds with Europe and the Middle East, as well as due to the good relations it maintains

President Demetris Christofias with the President of the European Commission José Manuel Barroso.

with its fellow EU member states and all the countries in the Middle East, Cyprus is ideally placed to act as a bridge between the two, in order to achieve a greater convergence of policies for the resolution of problems in the Euro-Mediterranean area. As a result, the European Union could benefit from Cyprus' close and excellent relations with the countries of the region, towards strengthening and enriching its relations and enhancing cooperation with the Mediterranean partners, as well as towards enhancing the Mediterranean dimension of the Union's policy priorities.

Cyprus fully supports the Union for the Mediterranean and actively participates in the relevant deliberations, so that this new body succeeds in fulfilling the high tasks assigned to it.

83

cyprus
in the world
the path to
eu membership

THE PATH TO EU MEMBERSHIP

In 1971 the government of Cyprus entered into negotiations with the European Economic Community that led to the signing on 19 December 1972 of an Association Agreement between the two parties. The aim of the Agreement was the establishment, in two stages and within a period of ten years, of a Customs Union between Cyprus and the EEC. The Agreement came into force on 1 June 1973.

On 4 July 1990, the Cyprus government submitted its application for membership to the European Communities. The European Commission issued its Opinion (Avis) on Cyprus' application on 30 June 1993.

The Opinion recognised the European identity and character of Cyprus and its vocation to belong to the Communities. It also confirmed that Cyprus satisfied the criteria for membership and was suitable to become a member of the Communities.

The Council of the EU discussed and endorsed the Opinion at its meeting on 4 October 1993. In its conclusions the Council also noted the following: «The Council supported the Commission's approach which was to propose, without awaiting a peaceful, balanced and lasting solution to the Cyprus problem, to use all the instruments offered by the Association Agreement to help, in close co-operation with the Cypriot government, with the economic, social and political transition of Cyprus towards integration into the European Union».

Meanwhile, the European Council, at its meetings in Corfu in June 1994 and again in Essen in December the same year, confirmed that Cyprus would be included in the next phase of enlargement.

On 6 March 1995, the EU General Affairs Council reaffirmed the suitability of Cyprus for accession and stipulated that accession negotiations with Cyprus would start six months after the conclusion of the 1996 Intergovernmental Conference.

Accession negotiations were formally launched on 31 March 1998; substantive negotiations began on 10 November 1998. By December 2002, Cyprus was the first of the candidate countries to complete accession negotiations according to the agreed road map. The sustained efforts for the timely completion of the accession negotiations culminated in the unprecedented and historic milestone decision, reached at the Copenhagen European Council in December 2003, to admit Cyprus, together with nine other countries, as a new member-state of the European Union.

The Treaty of Accession was signed in Athens on 16 April 2003 and came into effect on 1 May 2004.

On 6 March 1995, the EU General Affairs Council reaffirmed the suitability of Cyprus for accession and stipulated that accession negotiations with Cyprus would start six months after the conclusion of the 1996 Intergovernmental Conference.

President Tassos Papadopoulos and
Foreign Minister George Iacovou sign
the Cyprus EU Accession Treaty, in
Athens, Greece (16 April 2003).

cyprus
in the world
member of the
european union

MEMBER OF THE EUROPEAN UNION

On 1 May 2004 the Republic of Cyprus became a full member of the EU completing a long journey that lasted more than three decades. The President of the Republic of Cyprus, Tassos Papadopoulos, signed the Accession Treaty on 16 April 2003 in Athens, Greece and on 14 July the House of Representatives ratified the Treaty of Accession unanimously. In a statement during celebrations marking Cyprus' accession, the President of Cyprus said:

"...Our great joy for our accession to the European Union is overshadowed by our grief because we could not celebrate this moment together with our Turkish Cypriot compatriots and our great disappointment for the absence of a solution to our national problem..."

"This moment signals a momentous milestone in Cyprus' history. It is the second most important historic landmark after the proclamation of the Republic of Cyprus forty-four years ago. This moment marks the successful conclusion of a long effort and the hopeful beginning of a new course and a new era for Cyprus.

As from this moment, the Republic of Cyprus formally becomes a Member of the European Union. It becomes a full, integral and inseparable member of the great European family.

Our great joy for our accession to the European Union is overshadowed by our grief because we could not celebrate this moment together with our Turkish Cypriot compatriots and our great disappointment for the absence of a solution to our national problem.

Our accession to the European Union does not create rights only. It entails also obligations and

Celebrations for the accession of Cyprus to the European Union (1 May 2004).

responsibilities. We will claim and we will enjoy those rights. At the same time we will fulfil our obligations and undertake our responsibilities. Our aim and ambition is not to be a recalcitrant Member of the Union, but a constructive and creative partner."

The European Union

cyprus
in the world
member of the
european union

One of the protocols on Cyprus that was annexed to the Treaty provides for the suspension of the application of the acquis in the northern, Turkish-occupied part of the island, to be lifted in the event of a solution. It also states that the EU is ready "to accommodate the terms of a settlement in line with the principles on which the EU is founded", and expresses the desire that the accession of Cyprus should benefit all Cypriots.

> Cyprus has a lot to benefit from EU membership. It also has a lot to offer as a member -state. The geographic position of the country, the healthy state of its economy, the devotion of the people to the ideals of the EU are all elements which enable Cyprus to contribute to the stability and welfare of the European family.

Furthermore, on 13 December 2007 the President of Cyprus, together with the other EU leaders, signed the Treaty of Lisbon amending the Treaty on European Union and the Treaty establishing the European Community. The Cyprus House of Representatives ratified the Treaty on 3 July 2008.

On 1 January 2008, Cyprus joined the Eurozone and adopted the Euro as its official currency.

Cyprus has always been a part of the European family of nations. Accession to the EU was a natural choice for Cyprus, one that was dictated by its culture and civilisation, its history, its European outlook and its traditions of democracy and freedom.

Cyprus has a lot to benefit from EU membership. It also has a lot to offer as a member-state. The geographic position of the country, the healthy state of its economy, the devotion of the people to the ideals of the EU are all elements which enable Cyprus to contribute to the stability and welfare of the European family, regardless of its small size.

European Council Meeting in Brussels (June 2010).

Situated at the intersection of important transport and communications routes linking Europe to the Middle East and Asia, Cyprus aspires to become the region's economic and financial operations centre, a major communications and transport hub, and a meeting place for peoples and cultures. With its advanced technical infrastructure and skilled human resources it can become a bridge from where European enterprises launch their activities. Moreover, it can act as a shield, protecting Europe from the threat of terrorism, the inflow of narcotics, illegal immigration, money laundering, and trafficking in human beings.

The process of EU enlargement demostrates the common determination of the peoples of Europe to come together in a Union that has become the driving force for the consolidation of stability, security, peace, democracy and sustainable growth in Europe and beyond. As a full member of the Union, Cyprus

EU2009.CZ

Summit EU - USA

Praha | Prague | 5. 4. 2009

President Demetris
Christofias at the
EU-USA summit in
Prague (5 April 2009).

is working actively with all other member-states in shaping the future development of Europe and in completing the ambitious project of European reunification and integration.

The EU has taken a firm position regarding the Cyprus problem, a position that respects the sovereignty, independence, territorial integrity and unity of the country, in accordance with the relevant UN resolutions and the high-level agreements between the two communities. While the UN Secretary-General's mission of good offices has provided the framework for a negotiated settlement of the Cyprus problem, the EU is now expected to assume a central role in assuring that any proposed settlement conforms to its principles and legal norms.

As President Demetris Christofias stated in his inaugural speech on 28 February 2008: "The European Union can and should play a role in the efforts to solve the Cyprus problem. We look forward to the solidarity of our European partners and we expect that they will contribute toward breaking the deadlock and solving the Cyprus problem."

The president also reiterated that Cyprus will be an active partner in the EU, noting that: "As a member of the European Union, the Republic of Cyprus will participate actively in developments in Europe, with the goal of realising the vision of a socially sensitive Europe. Cyprus can become a bridge between Europe and the countries in our region and also with countries with which our island maintains relations within the ranks of the non-aligned movement."

Farewell to the last British Governor of Cyprus Sir Hugh Foot (16 August 1960).

political system and
administration

- THE SYMBOLS OF THE REPUBLIC OF CYPRUS
- THE POLITICAL LANDSCAPE
- EXECUTIVE
- LEGISLATIVE
- JUDICIARY
- INDEPENDENT OFFICERS AND BODIES
- DISTRICT ADMINISTRATION
- LOCAL AUTHORITIES

political system and
administration
the symbols of the
republic of Cyprus

THE FLAG

The flag of the Republic of Cyprus was defined in 1960 when Cyprus became an independent sovereign state.

Colours of the Flag: The background is white with a copper-coloured (pantone 1385 C) silhouette of the map of Cyprus in the center of the flag above two crossed olive-green-coloured (pantone 574 C) olive branches.

The copper colour has a dual symbolism: first, the name of the island is said to derive from the Greek word for copper; and second, copper is closely associated with Cyprus since antiquity when the island became a major producer and supplier of this mineral resource. The olive branches symbolize the hope for peace on the island.

THE EMBLEM

Colours of the Emblem: The background is white. The shield is copper-coloured (pantone 1385 C) while the dove inside the shield is white as are the olive branch in the mouth of the dove and the number "1960" underneath the dove.

The crossed olive branches bracing the shield are olive-green-coloured (pantone 574 C).

The dove and the olive branches symbolize the hope for peace on the island and the number "1960" refers to the year of the independence of Cyprus.

political system and
administration
the political landscape

THE POLITICAL LANDSCAPE

Cyprus is an independent, sovereign Republic with a presidential system of government. The constitution provides for separate executive, legislative and judicial branches of government with independent powers. The President is both Head of State and government.

EXECUTIVE

Executive power is exercised by the President (and Vice-President) through a Council of Ministers appointed by the President (and the Vice-President), who have the right of final veto on decisions of the Council of Ministers and laws or decisions of the House of Representatives concerning foreign affairs, defence and security.

According to the Constitution the President is to be Greek Cypriot elected by the Greek Cypriot community and the Vice-President is to be Turkish Cypriot elected by the Turkish Cypriot community, by universal suffrage for a five-year term of office.

According to the Constitution the President is to be Greek Cypriot elected by the Greek Cypriot community and the Vice-President is to be Turkish Cypriot elected by the Turkish Cypriot community, by universal suffrage for a five-year term of office. Moreover, thirty percent of the Ministries in the government were reserved for Turkish Cypriots to be appointed by the Vice-President. In December 1963, however, the Turkish Cypriot Vice-President and the three Turkish Cypriot ministers withdrew from the government. Since then, the government has been functioning by necessity only with Greek Cypriots in all ministries. The post of Vice-President remains vacant.

President Makarios and Vice-President Kutchuk cracking Easter eggs a custom of the Greek Orthodox religion (14 April 1963).

The Presidential Palace in the capital city, Nicosia.

95

The Council of Ministers exercises executive power in all matters. Each Minister is the head of his or her Ministry and exercises executive power on all matters within that Ministry's domain.

Ministerial portfolios include: Defence; Agriculture, Natural Resources and the Environment; Justice and Public Order; Commerce, Industry and Tourism; Foreign Affairs; Labour and Social Insurance; Interior; Finance; Education and Culture; Communications and Works; and Health.

The Government Spokesman and the Deputy Minister to the President are also present at the meetings of the Council of Ministers.

Council of Ministers meeting (8 April 2010).

The Ministry of Foreign Affairs.

The Ministry of Finance.

97

**Presidents and Vice-Presidents
of the Republic of Cyprus** (1960-2010)

Archbishop Makarios III
The first President of the
Republic of Cyprus was
elected in December 1959
and assumed office in 1960.
After his term of office had
expired in 1965 and had
been extended to 1968,
Makarios was re-elected in
1968 and 1973. He served
until his death in 1977.

Dr. Fazil Kutchuk
He was elected as the
first Vice-President of
the Republic of Cyprus
in December 1959 and
assumed office in 1960. He
served until December 1963,
when the Turkish Cypriot
community withdrew from
the government. Ever since
the post of Vice-President
remains vacant. He passed
away in 1984.

Spyros Kyprianou
He was elected in 1977
to serve for the remainder
of the term of President
Makarios, who died in
August of that year. He was
re-elected in 1978 and in
1983 and served until 1988.
He passed away in 2002.

George Vassiliou
He was elected in 1988 and
served until 1993.

Glafkos Clerides
He was first elected in 1993
and was re-elected in 1998.
He served until 2003.

Tassos Papadopoulos
He was elected in 2003
and served until 2008. He
passed away in 2008.

Demetris Christofias
He was elected in 2008.
His term of office
expires in 2013.

LEGISLATIVE

Legislative authority is exercised by a unicameral House of Representatives. Its members are elected for a five-year term. At the time of its establishment the House consisted of 50 members, 35 of whom were to be Greek Cypriots and 15 Turkish Cypriots.

Through a constitutional amendment in 1985 the number of seats was increased to 80, 56 allocated to Greek Cypriot members and 24 reserved for Turkish Cypriot deputies.

Following the withdrawal of the Turkish Cypriot members in 1964, the House has been functioning only with the Greek Cypriot members. The Maronite, Armenian and Latin religious groups, which vote as part of the Greek Cypriot community, elect one additional representative each from their ranks. These non-voting representatives attend meetings but do not participate in the House deliberations. They are consulted in matters concerning affairs of particular interest to their respective religious group.

For general election purposes, Cyprus is divided into six electoral districts, which correspond to the Republic's administrative districts. The current electoral law provides for a simple proportional representation system. Each voter can choose a party or an independent candidate, without having the

> Each voter can choose a party or an independent candidate, without having the option of selecting candidates from different parties. Seats are distributed according to the electoral strength of each party.

The House of Representatives.

100

Plenary of the House of Representatives.

option of selecting candidates from different parties. Seats are distributed according to the electoral strength of each party.

The sessions of the House are usually held every Thursday and are open to the public. The quorum of the House consists of at least one third of the total number of its members.

Beyond its legislative functions, the House of Representatives has developed significant relations and activities on the European and broader international scene. These include bilateral relations with other national parliaments, as well as relations with and/or participation in European and international parliamentary organisations.

Beyond its legislative functions, the House of Representatives has developed significant relations and activities on the European and broader international scene.

Under the Constitution, the President of the House is elected by the Representatives at the beginning and for the entire period of the term of office of the House of Representatives. In case of temporary absence or pending the filling of a vacancy of the office of the President of the House, the functions thereof are performed by the eldest Representative unless the Representatives decide otherwise.

Since the vacancy of the Vice-President's office in 1964, the President of the House serves as Acting President of the Republic in the absence or temporary incapacity of the President of the Republic. The President of the Republic is invested in office by the House of Representatives.

President of the European Commission Romano Prodi addresses the Cyprus House of Representatives (26 October 2001).

President of the European Parliament Josep Borrel Fontelles addresses the Cyprus House of Representatives (4 October 2005).

US Vice-President Lyndon Johnson addresses the Cyprus House of Representatives (31 August 1962).

Glafkos Clerides
He served from 1960 to
1976.

Tassos Papadopoulos
He served between July
and September 1976.
He passed away in 2008.

Spyros Kyprianou
He was first elected in
1976 and served until
1977. He served for a
second term from 1996
to 2001. He passed
away in 2002.

Alecos Michaelides
He served from 1977
to 1981. He passed
away in 2008.

George Ladas
He served from 1981
to 1986. He passed
away in 1997.

Vassos Lyssarides
He served from 1986
to 1991.

Alexis Galanos
He served from 1991
to 1996.

Demetris Christofias
He was first elected in
2001 and was re-elected
in 2006. He served until
his election as President
of the Republic of Cyprus
in February 2008.

Marios Garoyian
He was elected in
March 2008 to serve the
remainder of the term
of his predecessor who
became President of
Cyprus. His term expires
in May 2011.

105

PARLIAMENTARY POLITICAL PARTIES

A multi-party political landscape, with parties covering the whole spectrum of political ideologies, ensures the functioning of a free and democratic system. Turkish Cypriot political parties have refused to participate in the Parliament since 1964.

Progressive Party of Working People - AKEL

A left-wing party, it was founded in 1941, as a successor to the Communist Party of Cyprus (KKK), based on Marxist-Leninist principles, taking into account current international political and economic developments. In the parliamentary elections of 21 May 2006, the party won 31,16% of the vote and 18 seats.
It is a member of the European United Left-Nordic Green Left in the European Parliament.

Democratic Rally - DISY

A centre-right party, it was founded in 1976 by Glafkos Clerides. In the elections of 21 May 2006, the party won 30,3 % of the vote and 18 seats.
It is a member of the European People's Party, the Christian Democrat International, the European Democrat Union and the International Democrat Union.

Democratic Party-DIKO

A centrist political party, it was founded in 1976 by the late Spyros Kyprianou. In the parliamentary elections of 21 May 2006, the party won 17,9% of the vote and 11 seats.
DIKO is a member of the Progressive Alliance of Socialists and Democrats in the European Parliament.

106

Movement of Social Democrats - EDEK
The party is the successor to the Socialist Party EDEK, founded in 1969 by Dr. Vassos Lyssarides. In the elections of 21 May 2006, the party won 8.9 % of the vote and 5 seats. It is a member of the European Socialist Party, the Progressive Alliance of Socialists and Democrats in the European Parliament and of the Socialist International.

European Party
This centre party, established in July 2005, was a founding member of the European Democratic Party (EPD). In the elections of 21 May 2006, the party won 5.7 % of the vote and 3 seats.

Ecological-Environmental Movement
Also calling itself the Cyprus Green Party, it was founded in March 1996 and it is a member of the European Federation of Green Parties. In the elections of 21 May 2006, the party won 2.0 % of the vote and 1 seat.

JUDICIARY

Under the Constitution the judiciary is established as a separate power, independent from the other two branches of the state and autonomous in its sphere of competencies, authority and jurisdiction.

Its independence entails:
- Assumption and exercise of jurisdiction by the judicial power in all matters naturally pertaining to the sphere of the judicial power.
- Autonomy of the judiciary in rule making and regulating the exercise of its jurisdictions.
- Institutionally entrenched independence of judges from the other two powers of the state, the executive and legislative.

Courts are organized on a two-tier system:

THE SUPREME COURT

The Supreme Court is the highest court in the Republic. It is composed of thirteen judges, one of whom is the President. The Supreme Court is the final appellate court of the Republic. It is also vested with jurisdiction to determine the constitutionality of laws, rules and regulations and has sole competence and exclusive jurisdiction to review the legality of acts, decisions or omissions emanating from the exercise of executive or administrative authority. Moreover, it is vested with original jurisdiction to issue writs known in English Law as prerogative writs; that is orders in the nature

> A law may entrust original jurisdiction to the Supreme Court in a particular field of law and such jurisdiction has been vested in the Supreme Court in admiralty matters.

Interior aspect of the Supreme Court.

of Habeas Corpus, Mandamus, Certiorari, Quo Warranto and Prohibition. A law may entrust original jurisdiction to the Supreme Court in a particular field of law and such jurisdiction has been vested in the Supreme Court in admiralty matters. The Supreme Court, as the Electoral Court, has the power to hear and determine petitions concerning the interpretation and application of the Electoral Laws of the Republic.

The Supreme Court.

The Nicosia District Court.

FIRST INSTANCE COURTS

The principal First Instance Courts are the District Courts operating in every district of the Republic with the exception of the occupied areas; composed of District Judges, Senior District Judges and Presidents of District Courts. The other First Instance Courts are: the Assize Courts, the Military Court, the Industrial Disputes Court, the Rent Control Courts and the Family Courts.

INDEPENDENT OFFICERS AND BODIES

Certain officers and bodies are independent and do not come under any ministry, while in recent years a great number of new institutions with independent functions have been established due to the accession of Cyprus to the European Union. These independent officers and bodies are: the Attorney-General and the Auditor-General who head the Law Office and Audit Office respectively; the Governor of the Central Bank of Cyprus; the Ombudsman (Commissioner for Administration); the Public Service Commission; the Education Service Commission; the Planning Bureau; the Treasury; the Commission for the Protection of Competition; the Office of the Commissioner of Electronic Communications and Postal Regulation; the Cyprus Energy Regulatory Authority; the Cyprus Agricultural Payments Organisation; the Office of the Commissioner for Personal Data Protection; the Cooperative Societies Supervision and Development Authority; the Internal Audit Service; the Office of the Commissioner for State Aid Control; the Tenders Review Authority; the Law Commissioner; the Cyprus Radio and Television Authority; the Cyprus Securities and Exchange Commission; the Commissioner for the Protection of Children's Rights; the Reviewing Authority of Refugees and the Tax Tribunal.

The Central Bank.

111

DISTRICT ADMINISTRATION

For administrative purposes Cyprus is divided into six administrative districts: Nicosia, Limassol, Pafos, Larnaka (in the government-controlled areas) and Famagusta and Kerynia (in the occupied areas).
Each district is administered by a District Officer, who is a senior civil servant answerable to the Ministry of Interior. District Officers are appointed by the government as local representatives and act as coordinators and liaisons for the activities of all ministries in the districts.

Apart from their institutional role pursuant to the Communities Law of 1999, the District Administrations coordinate, guide and implement projects for the development of the communities. Furthermore, they play a significant role in the preparation, revision and modification of the local plans and policy statement, as well as in the process of the examination of objections.

The government provides administrative and technical support to most of the community councils and councils of community complexes through the civil servants serving in the District Administrations. District Administrations, with their diverse and multidimensional activity, aim at serving the public with the provision of ordinary administrative services, in accordance to the relevant laws and regulations, as well as implementing various rural development projects.

> District Administrations, with their diverse and multidimensional activity, aim at serving the public with the provision of ordinary administrative services, in accordance to the relevant laws and regulations, as well as implementing various rural development projects.

The Limassol District Administration offices.

LOCAL AUTHORITIES

There are two types of local authorities in Cyprus, municipalities and communities, which are governed by separate laws. In principle, municipalities constitute the form of local government in urban and tourist centres, while communities constitute the local structure in rural areas.

district
administration

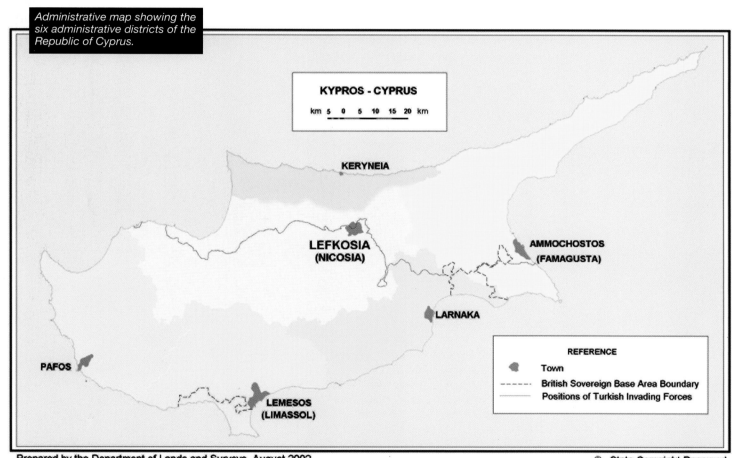

Administrative map showing the
six administrative districts of the
Republic of Cyprus.

KYPROS - CYPRUS

km 5 0 5 10 15 20 km

KERYNEIA

LEFKOSIA
(NICOSIA)

AMMOCHOSTOS
(FAMAGUSTA)

LARNAKA

PAFOS

LEMESOS
(LIMASSOL)

REFERENCE

Town

- - - - - British Sovereign Base Area Boundary

———— Positions of Turkish Invading Forces

Prepared by the Department of Lands and Surveys, August 2002

© State Copyright Reserved

MUNICIPALITIES

Any community may become a municipality by local referendum, subject to the approval of the Council of Ministers, provided it has either a population of more than 5.000, or has the economic resources to function as a municipality.

Since the Turkish invasion of 1974 and the subsequent occupation of the northern part of Cyprus, nine municipalities, although still maintaining their legal status, have been temporarily relocated to the free areas.

Mayors are elected directly by the citizens on a separate ballot, for a term of five years. The mayor is the executive authority of the municipality.

> Municipal councils, which are the policy-making bodies of municipalities, are elected directly by the citizens for a term of five years, but separately from the mayor. The council appoints the members of the administrative committee.

Municipal councils, which are the policy-making bodies of municipalities, are elected directly by the citizens for a term of five years, but separately from the mayor. The council appoints the members of the administrative committee. The latter's duties include the preparation of the municipality's budgets and annual financial statements, the provision of assistance and advice to the mayor in the execution of his duties, coordination of the work of other committees appointed by the council and the discharge of any other duties entrusted to it by the council or the mayor.

The main responsibilities of municipalities are the construction, maintenance and lighting of streets, the collection, disposal and treatment of waste, the

The Kyrenia Municipality Town Hall (temporarily in Nicosia since the 1974 Turkish occupation of Cyprus).

protection and improvement of the environment and the good appearance of the municipal areas, the construction, development and maintenance of municipal gardens and parks and the protection of public health. The Municipal Council has the authority to promote, when fiscally feasible, a vast range of activities and events, including the arts, education, sports and social services. In addition to the Municipalities Law, there are several laws giving municipalities additional important powers.

The main sources of revenue of municipalities are municipal taxes, fees and duties including the following: professional tax, immovable property tax, hotel accommodation tax, permit and licence fees,

The Nicosia Town Hall.

115

fees for refuse collection, fines. They also receive state subsidies. Taxes, duties and fees represent the major source, while state grants and subsidies amount to only a small percentage of revenue. The central government, however, usually finances major infrastructure projects undertaken by the municipalities.

COMMUNITIES

The functions of communities are generally similar to those of municipalities, although structurally different. The residents of the community elect the President of the Community and the Community Council for a five-year term. With the exception of some communities which are financially better off, the government provides essential administrative and technical assistance as well as most of the necessary services to most communities, through its District Offices. The revenue of Communities consists of state subsidies as well as taxes and fees collected from the residents of the area.

The community councils are responsible for the provision community services, water supply, and the regulation of professional practices.

In exercising their competencies, the councils enjoy a degree of independence, but as Local Authorities which exercise their competency in accordance to the relevant Law, they are normally subject to legal scrutiny and control by government bodies, and to control in serious matters such as the compulsory acquisition of real estate for municipal purposes and the signing of agreements exceeding five years.

The community councils are responsible for the provision community services, water supply, and the regulation of professional practices.

Lefkara village in the Larnaka district.

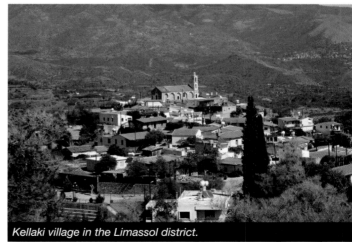
Kellaki village in the Limassol district.

Alona village in the Nicosia district.

Despite the broad range of competencies invested to community councils by the Communities Law adopted in 1999, the strategic goal of the government is to broaden further these competencies and at the same time the economic self-sufficiency of community councils so that they can respond in a timely and effective manner to the contemporary needs of the rural population.

people and
nature

- DEMOGRAPHY
- RELIGIOUS GROUPS
- TOWNS
- GEOGRAPHY
- CLIMATE
- FLORA AND FAUNA

people and nature

DEMOGRAPHY

The population of the Republic of Cyprus is 885.600 (December 2008) of whom 668.700 belong to the Greek Cypriot community, (75,5%), 88.700 (10%) to the Turkish Cypriot community and 128.200 (14,5%) are foreign citizens residing in Cyprus.

GREEK AND TURKISH CYPRIOT COMMUNITIES

The language of the Greek Cypriot community, whose presence on the island dates back to the second half of the second millennium BC, is Greek and the community adheres predominantly to the Autocephalous Greek Orthodox Church of Cyprus.

The language of the Turkish Cypriot community is Turkish and the members of the community are Sunni Muslims. The original nucleus of the Turkish Cypriot community in Cyprus were soldiers of the Ottoman army that conquered the island in 1571 and of immigrants from Turkey brought in by the firman (decree) of Sultan Selim II. Gradually, the island evolved into a demographic mosaic of Greek and Turkish villages, as well as many mixed communities. The extent of this symbiosis could be seen in the participation of the two groups in commercial and religious fairs, pilgrimages to each other's shrines, and the occurrence, albeit rare, of intermarriage.

> Gradually, the island evolved into a demographic mosaic of Greek and Turkish villages, as well as many mixed communities.

Armenians, Maronites and Latins are recognised by the Constitution of the Republic of Cyprus (Article 2 § 3) as "religious groups" and, according to a

The Archbishop of Cyprus, Chrysostomos II and Mr Ahmet Yonluer, Turkish Cypriot Director of Religious Affairs, during a meeting hosted by the President of the Council of Europe Parliamentary Assembly Rene van der Linden at the Ledra Palace hotel in Nicosia (22 February 2007).

referendum held on 13 November 1960, all three opted to belong to the Greek-Cypriot community, thus voting as part of that community. The members of these groups enjoy, of course, fully the same benefits as other community members and are eligible for public service and official positions of the Republic.

The Ayios Ioannis Greek Orthodox Cathedral in Nicosia, dedicated to St John the Baptist.

The Hala Sultan Tekke, near the Salt Lake in Larnaka, is considered to be the most important religious shrine for Muslims on the island.

The Arablar mosque and the Panayia Phaneromeni church next to each other in Nicosia.

121

POPULATION BY ETHNIC GROUP

The population of Cyprus by ethnic group at independence in 1960 and in 1973, the last year before the Turkish invasion, as well as in December 2008, was as follows:

	1960 (Census)		**1973** (Census)		**2008** (December)	
	Number	%	Number	%	Number	%
Greek Cypriot Community(1)	447.901	78,20	498.511	78,9	668.700	75,5
Turkish Cypriot Community	103.822	18,13	116.000	18,4	88.700	10
Others:	20.984	3,66	17.267	2,7	128.200	14,5
Total:	572.207	100,00	631.778	100,00	885.600	100,00

1) According to the 1960 Constitution, the small religious groups of Maronites, Armenians and Latins opted to be classified demographically within the Greek Cypriot community. They are hence presented as one total.
Sources: *Census of Population and Agriculture 1961, Vol. 1, and Demographic Report 1987, Department of Statistics and Research.*

In 1960, when Cyprus became an independent country, its estimated population was 574.000, the ratio of Greek Cypriots to Turkish Cypriots being about 82:18. When the 1963 intercommunal crisis broke out, the Turkish Cypriots were living interspersed throughout the island, as before, with no majority or particular concentration in any administrative district. There were Turkish Cypriot quarters in all the main cities. Of the villages, 392 were exclusively Greek Cypriot, 123 Turkish Cypriot, and 114 of mixed population, all three types of villages being situated throughout the island.

The Census of 1973 showed the population of Cyprus to be 631.778, giving an average rate of growth of 0,8% between 1960 and 1973. The ethnic distribution of the population did not change over this period and

the proportion of each community remained stable while birth rates declined and Cyprus lost a part of the natural increase of its population through emigration.

The impact of Turkey's military invasion on the population was devastating. The Greek Cypriots living in what is now the occupied area, about one third of the total Greek Cypriot community, were forced by the Turkish troops to flee to the southern government-controlled area, while the Turkish Cypriots, who were scattered throughout the island, were compelled by Turkey to move to the Turkish occupied area in the north. This was part of Turkey's policy to cleanse the area under its military control of the presence of ethnic Greeks, and to impose a total segregation of the two communities. After the invasion, the total population also declined and for a number of years remained below the figure of 1974. Gradually, with birth, death and emigration rates of Greek Cypriots becoming more normal, the population picked up and started growing again. Even so, it was only by the end of 1984 that finally the total population of Cyprus exceeded the highest figure reached in mid-1974. However, while the population of Greek Cypriots increased gradually since 1976, and at a faster rate since 1990 due to the repatriation of Greek Cypriots, the population of the Turkish Cypriot community has been decreasing since 1985. This difference in the population growth of the two communities is exclusively due to differing migration movements, as both fertility and mortality are about the same for the two communities.

Demographic analysis and examination of the statistical data on arrivals and departures of Turkish Cypriots, as well as Turks from Turkey, clearly show a fall in the number of indigenous Turkish Cypriots due to their emigration abroad and their replacement by an even greater number of illegal settlers from Turkey.

According to statistical evidence, press reports and comments by Turkish Cypriot politicians, Turkish Cypriots, faced with the problems of unemployment, economic uncertainty and pressure from the illegal Turkish settlers who are given many privileges, continue to emigrate. It is estimated that about 58.000 Turkish Cypriots emigrated in the period 1974-2005.

Given the continuing reports of emigration of Turkish Cypriots and the fact that the population increase in the occupied areas every year is greater than the birth and death rates would justify, it is obvious that the number of illegal settlers from Turkey is much higher than that of the indigenous Turkish Cypriots.

According to estimates of the Cyprus government Statistical Service, which are also supported by statements by Turkish Cypriot politicians, the number of settlers from Turkey is currently estimated at around 160.000, while the Turkish Cypriot population is estimated at about 88.700. During 2004-2005 alone, it is estimated that about 43.000 settlers were transferred from Turkey to the Turkish occupied areas of Cyprus.

During 2004-2005 alone, it is estimated that about 43.000 settlers were transferred from Turkey to the Turkish occupied areas of Cyprus.

The Holy Cross Catholic church in Nicosia in the early 1950s.

Mass at the Holy Cross Catholic church.

His Holiness Pope Benedict XVI at the Holy Cross Catholic church (5 June 2010).

RELIGIOUS GROUPS

The Law on Religious Groups states that each religious group is represented in the House of Representatives by an elected Representative. The participation of the Representatives, who act as a liaison between their respective group and the state, has a consultative nature. They enjoy the same privileges as other MPs, they participate in the Parliamentary Committee on Education and they attend the plenary meetings of the House. Although they can express their views on matters relating to their respective religious group, they do not vote. The voting representatives of the religious groups are those elected by the entire Greek Cypriot community, where these groups belong.

LATINS

The first Latin Archbishopric in Cyprus was established in Nicosia in 1196 during the Frankish rule on the island. However, the present Latin community of the island, as regards both its clerical and secular members, came into being during the early Ottoman period and it began to increase notably in numbers during the late Ottoman and early British periods. It had a nationally heterogeneous composition, with its members originating from Venice, other areas of Italy, Malta, France and even Dalmatia. Most of the Latins on the island not belonging to the clergy were engaged in commercial pursuits, but nonetheless also developed notable initiatives in other fields such as agriculture and education, and thereby made a significant contribution to the life of the island. The religious leader of the group is a Partiarchal Vicar General accountable to the Latin Patriarch of Jerusalem and ex officio representative of the Holy See pro-Nuncio in Jerusalem.

The Latins of Cyprus form a compact but steadily increasing community differing markedly from the Armenians and the Maronites insofar as they are not nationally homogeneous. Today, it is estimated that traditional Latins number about 1.000 persons, while the last 25-30 years have seen the arrival of thousands of Roman Catholics from countries of the former Soviet bloc, western Europe, south – east Asia and Latin America.

ARMENIANS

The presence of Armenians on the island dates back as early as the sixth century, while the number of Armenians in Cyprus significantly increased following the massive forced deportations from Ottoman Turkey and the massacres and genocide they suffered by the Ottoman Turks during the late nineteenth and early twentieth centuries. According to the Constitution (Article 2 § 3), the Armenian-Cypriots are recognised as a religious group, while the Western Armenian language is recognised and protected by the Cyprus government as a "minority language," according to the provisions of the European Charter for Regional or Minority Languages. The religious leader of the group, the Archbishop, is accountable to the Catholicos of the Great House of Cilicia in Antelias. Currently, Armenian-Cypriots, who number about 3.500 people, live mostly in the urban areas of Nicosia, Larnaka and Limassol. Through their churches, schools, clubs, radio programme, monthly newspapers and websites they try to preserve their very rich cultural heritage, language and religion. As a result of the 1974 Turkish invasion, the Armenians lost significant properties, such as the Sourp Magar Armenian Monastery in the Halefka area and the Ganchvor Sourp Asdvadzadzin Monastery in Famagusta, a primary school and church in Nicosia, and several other vital sites and assets.

Today, there are three Armenian churches and primary schools in Cyprus, one of each in each town. In addition, the Armenians have a secondary school in Nicosia, the world renowned Melkonian Educational Institute, which was established in 1926 by the Melkonian brothers and was the only remaining boarding school servicing students of the Armenian Diaspora from nearly forty countries. It is currently not in operation.

The Nareg Armenian elementary school in Nicosia.

The Melkonian Educational Institute in Nicosia.

The Sourp Magar (Saint Makarios) Armenian Monastery in the occupied part of Cyprus.

The Maronite Cathedral of Our Lady of Graces in Nicosia.

The St Maron Elementary School in Anthoupolis.

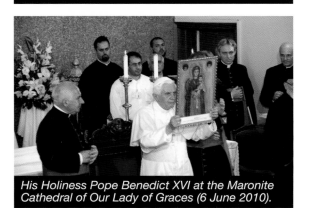

His Holiness Pope Benedict XVI at the Maronite Cathedral of Our Lady of Graces (6 June 2010).

MARONITES

The Maronites derive their name from Saint Maron (350-410 AD) who lived in the region of Apameus in "Syria Secunda", an administrative division of the Byzantine Empire. The history of the Maronites in Cyprus goes back many centuries. Maronites moved to Cyprus from the ancient territories of Syria, the Holy Land and Lebanon in four principal migrations between the eighth and the thirteenth centuries. The Maronites who now live in Cyprus consider themselves of Lebanese origin and they are Christian Catholics. They have a Maronite Archbishop who is elected by the Holy Synod of the Maronite Church in Lebanon and confirmed by His Holiness the Pope. Although the Maronites are educated in Greek schools and speak fluent Greek, they have their own language, they practice their own Catholic Maronite religion, they use the Aramaic language in their liturgy and they have their own culture and customs. The Cypriot Maronite Arabic Language has been earmarked for protection by the Republic of Cyprus under the European Charter for Regional or Minority Languages. In 1960, the Maronites living in Cyprus were approximately 2.750, living mainly in the four villages of Kormakitis, Asomatos, Karpashia and Ayia Marina. As a result of the Turkish invasion in 1974, most Maronites were displaced and became refugees, whereas a small number remained enclaved in the three Maronite villages of Kormakitis, Asomatos and Karpashia. Today, there are about one hundred enclaved Maronites, while it is estimated that Maronites number about 6.000 persons living all over the island.

NICOSIA

The capital of the island is Nicosia with a population of 234.200 in the sector controlled by the Cyprus government. It is situated roughly in the centre of the island and is the seat of government as well as the main business centre. It is currently the only divided capital in the world, due to Turkey's military occupation of part of Cyprus. Nicosia is a sprawling cosmopolitan city as well as a commercial centre. The old city is quaint, surrounded by Venetian Walls built in the sixteenth century, with narrow streets, sidewalk tavernas, restored buildings and tourist shops that bring history to life.

LIMASSOL

The second largest town is Limassol, on the south coast, with a population of around 185.100 inhabitants. Since Turkey's invasion of Cyprus in 1974, it has become the island's chief port, an industrial centre and an important tourist resort. Limassol is a bustling town with ten miles of coastline filled with restaurants, tavernas and night spots. It is home to two popular annual events, the Carnival and the Wine Festival.

LARNAKA

Larnaka, also on the south coast of the island, has a population of 82.700 and is the country's second commercial port and an important tourist resort. The Larnaka International Airport is located to the south of the city. The birthplace of the philosopher Zenon, Larnaka is famous for its Palm Tree Promenade overlooking the sea. It was in Larnaka that Saint Lazarus came to live after his resurrection by Christ. The Cathedral of Saint Lazarus is a magnificent building.

PAFOS

Pafos, on the south-west coast, with a population of 55.900, is a fast-developing tourist resort, home to the island's second international airport and an attractive fishing harbour. With an abundance of historic sites and fine beaches, the whole town of Pafos is included on the official UNESCO world heritage list of cultural and national treasures.

OCCUPIED TOWNS

The towns of Famagusta, Kyrenia and Morfou as well as part of Nicosia, have been under military occupation since the invasion of Cyprus by Turkey in 1974. The Greek Cypriot inhabitants of these towns were forced to flee to the southern, government-controlled area of the island. The Turkish authorities installed illegal settlers in their homes and properties, brought in mostly from Anatolia, Turkey.

The Turkish occupied town of Famagusta.

The harbour in the Turkish occupied town of Kyrenia.

The church of Ayios Mamas in the Turkish occupied town of Morfou.

137

GEOGRAPHY

Cyprus is the third largest island in the Mediterranean, after Sicily and Sardinia, with an area of 9.251 sq. kms (3.572 sq. miles).

It is situated at the north-eastern corner of the Mediterranean, at a distance of 300 km north of Egypt, 90 km west of Syria, and 60 km south of Turkey. Greece lies 360 km to the north-west (Rhodes-Karpathos).

The country has two mountain ranges: the Pentadaktylos range which runs along almost the entire northern coast, and the Troodos massif in the central and south-western parts of the island. Cyprus' coastal line is indented and rocky in the north with long sandy beaches in the south. The north coastal plain, covered with olive and carob trees, is backed by the steep and narrow Pentadaktylos mountain range of limestone, rising to a height of 1.042 m. In the south, the extensive mountain massif of Troodos, covered with pine, dwarf oak, cypress and cedar, culminates in the peak of Mount Olympus, 1.953 m. above sea level. Between the two ranges lies the fertile plain of Messaoria. Cyprus is almost surrounded by coastal valleys where the soil is suitable for agriculture. Arable land constitutes 46.8 percent of the total area of the island. There are no rivers, only torrents which flow after heavy rain.

> Cyprus' coastal line is indented and rocky in the north with long sandy beaches in the south.

The Pentadaktylos mountain range.

The Tzelefos bridge, Troodos mountains.

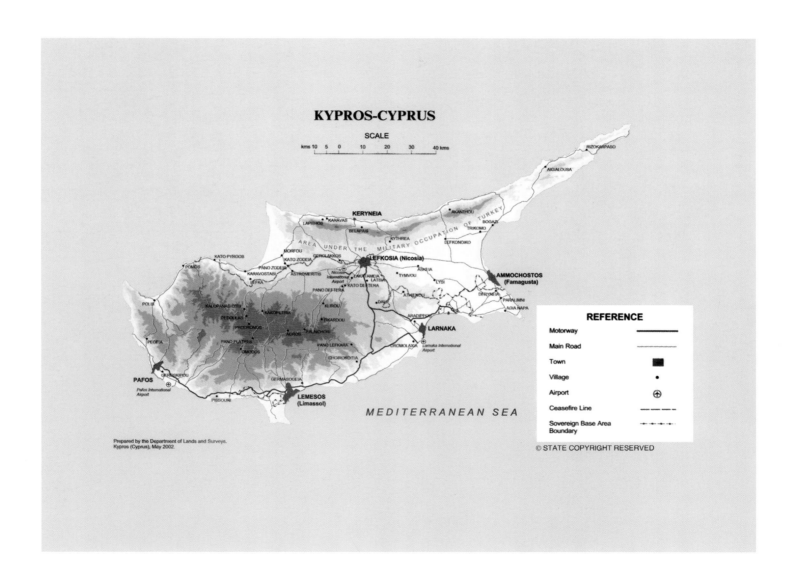

KYPROS-CYPRUS

SCALE

kms 10 5 0 10 20 30 40 kms

RIZOKARPASO

AIGIALOUSA

KERYNEIA

AKANTHOU

LAPITHOS
KARAVAS
BELAPAIS
KYTHREA
BOGAZI
TRIKOMO

AREA   UNDER   THE   MILITARY   OCCUPATION   OF   TURKEY

LEFKONOIKO

KATO PYRGOS
MORFOU
KATO ZODEIA
GEROLAKKOS
PANO ZODEIA
ASTROMERITIS
POMOS
KARAVOSTASI
LEFKA
LEFKOSIA (Nicosia)

ASKEIA
AMMOCHOSTOS
(Famagusta)

Nicosia
International
Airport
LAKATAMEIA
LATSIA
TYMVOU
LYSI

PANO DEFTERA
KATO DEFTERA
KATO DEFTERA
POLIS
KALOPANAGIOTIS
KAKOPETRIA
KLIROU
DALI
DEROYNEIA
PARALIMNI

PEDOULAS
PIKARDOU
ATHIENOU
AGIA NAPA

PEGEIA
PRODROMOS
PALAICHORI
ARADIPPOU

PANO PLATRES
AGROS

PANO LEFKARA

GEROSKIPOU
DIKOMOS
CHOIROKOITIA

PAFOS
PISSOURI
GERMASOGEIA
DROMOLAXIA
LARNAKA
Larnaka International
Airport

Pafos International
Airport

LEMESOS
(Limassol)

MEDITERRANEAN SEA

Prepared by the Department of Lands and Surveys.
Kypros (Cyprus), May 2002.

REFERENCE

Motorway	————
Main Road	————
Town	■
Village	•
Airport	⊕
Ceasefire Line	— — —
Sovereign Base Area Boundary	+—+—+

CLIMATE

Cyprus has a Mediterranean climate: hot, dry summers from June to September and mild, wet winters from November to March, which are separated by short Autumn and Spring seasons of rapid change in weather patterns in October, April and May.

Sunshine is abundant during the whole year, particularly from April to September when the daily average exceeds eleven hours. Winds are on the whole light to moderate. Gales are very infrequent and heavy storms rare.

Snow hardly falls in the lowlands and on the northern range, but is a frequent feature every winter on ground above 1.000 metres in the Troodos range. From December till April snow is usually in evidence there, but hardly continuous. Yet, during the coldest months it lies in considerable depth for several weeks, attracting skiers.

Snow hardly falls in the lowlands and on the northern range, but is a frequent feature every winter on ground above 1.000 metres in the Troodos range.

climate

The Nissi beach in Ayia Napa.

FLORA AND FAUNA

With its approximately 1.800 species, subspecies and varieties of flowering plants, Cyprus is an extremely interesting place for nature lovers and has all the attributes which make it a botanist's paradise. Being an island, it is sufficiently isolated to allow the evolution of a strong endemic flowering element. At the same time, being surrounded by big continents, it incorporates botanological elements of the neighbouring land masses. About seven percent of the indigenous plants of the island - 140 different species and subspecies - are endemic to Cyprus. The Cyclamen (Cyclamen cyprium) has been declared Cyprus' national plant while the Golden oak (Quercus alnifolia) has become the island's national tree.

> About seven percent of the indigenous plants of the island - 140 different species and subspecies - are endemic to Cyprus.

Golden Oak (Quercus alnifolia).

The best period of the year to study the native flora, especially the herbaceous plants, is spring, but also winter in the lowlands, where the flowering season begins early with the first rains. On the mountains and along main streams this period is extended.

Cultivated plants on the lowlands include cereals, irrigated crops of various vegetables (potatoes, tomatoes, etc.), whereas citrus species are commonly cultivated along the coastal zone. Olive, carob, and almond trees constitute a major component of cultivated plants at low and mid altitudes. At medium altitudes, vineyards are dominant in many places, especially in the Limassol and Pafos Districts. At higher elevations, in addition to vineyards, there are orchards of apple, cherry and peach trees.

Citrus fruit.

Tulipa cypria.

Forest vegetation on state and private land covers about 42% of the total area of the island (about 18.5% are high forests and 23.5% are other wooded land). They are natural forests consisting mainly of Calabrian pine (Pinus brutia) and Black pine (Pinus nigra ssp. Pallasiana), which covers the higher slopes of the Troodos Range. Other species include the Cypress, Juniper, Plane tree and Alder. Endemic species include the Golden oak (Quercus alnifolia) which is restricted on the Troodos mountain range, and Cedar (Cedrus brevifolia), which is restricted around the Tripylos area in the Pafos Forest. The forests of Cyprus are an important national resource. They provide timber and non-wood products and contribute significantly to the beauty of the landscape, the preservation of the national heritage, the protection of water supplies, and contribute to the economic development of village communities. Forests also attract visitors from foreign countries, in this way contributing to the national economy.

> Forests attract visitors from foreign countries, in this way contributing to the national economy.

Pinus brutia forest, Troodos mountains.

Orchis anatolica.

145

Green turtle (Chelonia Mydas).

The present-day fauna of Cyprus includes some 7 species of land mammals, 26 species of amphibians and reptiles, 365 species of birds, and a great variety of insects, while the coastal waters of the island give shelter to 197 fish species and various species of crabs, sponges and echinodermata.

The largest wild animal that still lives on the island is the Cyprus moufflon (Ovis orientalis ophion), a rare type of wild sheep that can only be found in Cyprus. Cyprus is used by millions of birds as a stopover during their migration from Europe to Africa and back. The main reason for that is the existence on the island of two wetlands, with unique and international importance, namely the Larnaka and Akrotiri salt lakes. From the numerous wild birds of Cyprus, birds of prey are the most fascinating and among them the Eleonora's falcon (Falco eleonorae) and the imperial eagle (Aquila heliaca) are the jewels in the crown. The island's sea creatures include seals and turtles. Two marine turtles, the Green turtle (Chelona mydas) and the Loggerhead turtle (Caretta caretta) breed regularly on the island's sandy beaches and are strictly protected.

> The largest wild animal that still lives on the island is the Cyprus moufflon, a rare type of wild sheep that can only be found in Cyprus.

Flamingos at the Larnaka Salt Lake.

Long-eared owl (Asio Otus).

Grass snake (Natrix natrix cypriaca).

Long-eared hedgehog (Hemiechinus auritus dorotheae).

The Cyprus moufflon (Ovis orientalis ophion).

147

economy

the economy

THE ECONOMY IN PERSPECTIVE
(1960-2010)

Dr Michael Sarris

During the fifty years since independence in 1960, Cyprus has been gradually transformed from a mostly closed economy, based on agriculture and mining, into a service-based, export-oriented economy. Independence did not only mark political liberation from British colonial rule, but also freed the creative spirit of the people of Cyprus, especially their entrepreneurial drive. In the early years, agricultural production shifted towards irrigated products for export such as oranges, potatoes, vegetables and grapes, but also animal husbandry for domestic consumption. The first years of industrialisation were concentrated on agricultural processing, soft drinks and tobacco, followed by products for the construction sector, clothing and shoes.

> During the fifty years since independence in 1960, Cyprus has been gradually transformed from a mostly closed economy, based on agriculture and mining, into a service-based, export-oriented economy.

Much of this transformation was achieved because of the open character of the economy, notwithstanding a policy of import substitution with relatively high tariff protection. A big step towards openness was made in 1973, when Cyprus signed a Customs Union agreement with the European Economic Community. Becoming part of the Customs Union was the first initiative towards joining the European Union (EU), thirty years later.

During the post independence period, fiscal policy remained prudent, with budget surpluses in ten out of the fourteen years leading to 1974 and only small deficits in the other four years. This period was also characterised by low inflation and modest current account deficits. The size of the public sector and of the civil service remained relatively stable. While the government adopted policies of indicative planning for its market oriented economy, there was little government involvement in the productive sectors. A major role for the government was to build a new, or to improve the existing infrastructure.

POST INVASION PERIOD

Apart from the immediate effects of the 1974 military invasion and occupation of more than a third of Cyprus by Turkey (war victims, massive displacement of the population, missing persons, loss of property), there was also a devastating impact on the economy, characterised by mass unemployment and the loss of a very significant part of the production capacity of the Cyprus economy. Particularly hit were the sectors of agriculture, tourism and agriculture-based industry. Light industry in other sectors, in the areas that remained under the control of the government of Cyprus, however, showed strong dynamism, helped by the rapidly growing Arab markets and the overall liberalisation of international trade.

> The tourism, shipping, electricity and telecommunications industries recorded remarkable growth. The banking sector, including the cooperative movement, also exhibited an impressive expansion.

An expansionary fiscal stance was followed as was appropriate in order to address the consequences of the invasion and subsequent occupation, especially through expenditures for infrastructure purposes. In parallel, there was a significant reduction in public and private sector wages. As would be expected, there was a sharp turnaround in public finances, with deficits around six percent of the Gross Domestic Product (GDP), increasing public debt and a build-up of inflationary pressures and external current account deficits.

The government also played a key role in trying to support the economic recovery through guarantees for enterprise loans and the significant expansion of the public payroll, while providing, at the same time,

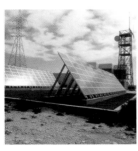

A mobile phone sub-station operating with solar energy.

a minimum standard of living for tens of thousands of refugees. Despite an increase in savings, there was a sharp increase in borrowing from abroad, leading to a much higher private and public (foreign) debt.

PATH TO RECOVERY

Led by the sacrifices of the working people and the entrepreneurial skills of the business community, there was a remarkable recovery of the economy relatively soon after the 1974 invasion. The mass unemployment created as a result of Turkey's military aggression, was transformed to near full employment within three years. Employment growth was mostly observed in the areas of construction and services. There was also strong encouragement of Cypriots to work abroad, especially in the construction industry in the Middle East/Arab countries, which absorbed large numbers of people from Cyprus.

During this period, the tourism, shipping, electricity and telecommunications industries recorded remarkable growth. The banking sector, including the cooperative movement, also exhibited an impressive expansion. Beginning in 1976, there was a dramatic increase in the number of offshore companies established in Cyprus, attracted by a favorable tax system in a number of services sectors, including shipping, banking, insurance, information technology, and consulting. Accounting and Law firms also played a major role in attracting these offshore companies, strengthening the otherwise modest direct employment creation impact of these companies.

The Agios Athanasios
fly-over, Limassol bypass.

153

THE GOLDEN ERA

The crisis in Lebanon and the sharp increase in oil prices, with the resulting expansion in the export markets and construction opportunities in the Arab world, were crucial for the recovery of the Cyprus economy after 1974. This has helped consolidate economic performance during the so called "golden era", with the Cyprus economy exhibiting robust economic growth, averaging around six percent, which was above the average trend of the EU. Moreover, trade was significantly expanded, as shown by the ratio of total trade to the GDP of around one. Private consumption, exports of services and, to a lesser extent, investment, were the main growth drivers. The unemployment rate remained remarkably stable and historically lower than the EU average unemployment rate, partly due to the fact that for long periods, growth was labour intensive.

Inflation was relatively contained due to prudent monetary and fixed exchange rate policies, fluctuating between two percent and three percent, except during the period of the oil shocks in 1970s. The combination of wage indexation and low unemployment, however, led to rapid wage expansion, which was faster than productivity gains.

Regarding the currency system, the Cyprus pound was pegged to the pound sterling until 1972 and then to a trade-weighted basket of currencies and from 1992 till 1999 to the European Currency Unit (ECU). This choice was guided mostly by the focus of this currency area on price and macroeconomic stability.

> Regarding the currency system, the Cyprus pound was pegged to the pound sterling until 1972 and then to a trade-weighted basket of currencies and from 1992 till 1999 to the European Currency Unit (ECU).

The services sector is acquiring increasing importance.

THE ROAD TO STABILITY

Although the link to the sterling and then to a currency basket aimed at minimising fluctuations in import and export prices, it also delivered price stability because trading partners were also committed to price stability. Furthermore, an unambiguous pegging of the exchange rate, even under the strain by the events in 1974 and the Exchange Rate Mechanism (ERM) crisis in 1992, ensured price stability. At the time, it was also recognised that a devaluation of the currency would not improve competitiveness, due to the resulting higher cost of imports and the existence of wage indexation.

The port of Limassol.

The road to stability was also ensured by the credibility and independence of the Central Bank, which was efficiently monitoring credit expansion and using current account deficits as indicators of inflationary pressures. The qualitative credit restraints imposed by the Central Bank, were used as tools for controlling threats towards imbalances. For example, the restraints imposed in 1980 aimed at containing inflation and in 1999 they aimed at preventing further problems in the stock market.

An important landmark was the creation of a framework of open market operations in the mid-1990s, which paved the ground for abolishing statutory interest rate ceilings and liberalising foreign borrowing, while a new Banking Law strengthened prudential and supervision rules. The years between 1999 and 2004, signalled a period of harmonisation and the abolition of several distortions for the efficient functioning of the markets, such as interest rate and capital movements liberalisation and the opening of the market in the utilities sectors to competition.

> The road to stability was also ensured by the credibility and independence of the Central Bank, which was efficiently monitoring credit expansion and using current account deficits as indicators of inflationary pressures.

THE EURO CHALLENGE

In 1999, the Cyprus pound was linked to the euro, again in the context of aiming at price stability, which was believed would be ensured because of the anti-inflation credentials of the European Central Bank (ECB). Five years later, in 2004, severe capital outflows called for sharp increases in interest rates

Cyprus Telecommunications Authority customer services.

to defend the Cyprus pound. This was reversed very soon thereafter during the run-up to Cyprus' EU accession, and especially the adoption of the euro, with strong capital inflows causing a housing bubble and resulting in an expansion in bank loan portfolios and household debt.

After successfully entering the Eurozone in 2008, the challenge for containing inflation fell primarily on fiscal policy and structural reforms, to foster productivity and preserve competitiveness. Moreover, fiscal consolidation must now be more ambitious than before the adoption of the euro, as monetary policy can no longer address imbalances at the national level.

A catering factory.

STRUCTURAL IMBALANCES
AND THE WORLD CRISIS

The world economic crisis brought to the surface major structural imbalances which need to be corrected, since they have a negative impact on the medium term prospects of the Cyprus economy. The most urgent challenge concerns public finances, which have deteriorated markedly in 2009 and are projected to worsen, if corrective measures are not taken. For example, a significant structural weakness is the size of the public sector, which has been steadily growing in the last years.

> Major events, such as the prospect of entering the World Trade Organisation (WTO), the European Customs Union, the EU and the Eurozone were intelligently used to anchor important and long-debated reforms.

The next most serious imbalance is the high current account deficit. Even though this imbalance has recently been reduced due to cyclical factors, resulting in a sharp reduction in imports, the competitiveness challenge of the economy still remains unresolved.

CONCLUSIONS

The Cyprus economy has performed remarkably well for most of the period since independence. It has weathered significant external shocks and has taken advantage of a number of different opportunities. A key driving force has been the openness and the responsiveness to international markets and a successful partnership between the private and public sectors. The government invested in infrastructure essential for growth, and the private sector exploited exogenous opportunities such as the crisis in Lebanon, and the expanding markets in the Arab World, Eastern Europe and Russia. Economic policies have been overall appropriate, though some times

uneven, providing a supportive framework of exchange rate and financial stability and expansionary fiscal policy when appropriate, all these resulting in reasonable price stability, strong employment growth and rising living standards.

Major events, such as the prospect of entering the World Trade Organisation (WTO), the European Customs Union, the

A pastry factory.

EU and the Eurozone were intelligently used to anchor important and long-debated reforms. Good industrial relations and economic migration underpinned a relatively manageable wage growth, and when wage growth outpaced productivity the transformation to a service economy accelerated.

Nevertheless, significant imbalances, which need urgent correction, remain: a structural fiscal deficit, a sizeable external account deficit, suggesting productivity and competitiveness shortcomings, a public sector that has grown too large and a medium-term challenge related to an ageing population.

Membership of the Eurozone provides important advantages but also calls for responsibilities. New markets mostly in emerging economies such as China, India and Brazil provide new opportunities. The quality of the economy in the future will depend on how these responsibilities and opportunities are handled.

Manufacturing of animal vitamins.

The power station at Moni.

BASIC ECONOMIC CHARACTERISTICS
Ministry of Finance

The economy of Cyprus can generally be characterised as small, open and dynamic, with services constituting its engine power. Since the accession of Cyprus to the European Union on 1 May 2004, its economy has undergone significant economic and structural reforms that have transformed the economic landscape. Interest rates have been liberalised, while price controls and investment restrictions have been lifted. Moreover, other wide-ranging structural reforms have been promoted, covering the areas of competition, the financial sector and the enterprise sector. Full liberalisation of the foreign direct investment regime in Cyprus has also been implemented. Moreover, a tax reform was implemented in 2002, which significantly lowered the tax rates.

> The major trading partners of Cyprus are the EU member-states, especially Greece and the United Kingdom, which are two countries which have been greatly affected by the crisis.

The services sector is the fastest growing area and accounted for about 80% of GDP in 2009. This development reflects the gradual restructuring of the Cypriot economy from an exporter of minerals and agricultural products in the period 1961-73 and an exporter of manufactured goods in the latter part of the 1970s and the early part of the 80s, to an international tourist, business and services centre during the 1980s, 1990s and the 2000s. The secondary sector (manufacturing) accounted for around 17.5% of GDP in 2009. The primary sector (agriculture and fishing) is continuously shrinking and only reached 2.5% of GDP in 2009.

The economy of Cyprus is open, as shown by the share of total imports and exports to GDP being around 106% in 2008. However, the percentage shrunk to around 88% in 2009, due to the impact of the international economic crisis. The major trading partners of Cyprus are the EU member-states, especially Greece and the United Kingdom, which are two countries which have been greatly affected by the crisis.

The private sector, which is dominated by small and medium-sized enterprises, has a leading role in the production process. On the other hand, the government's role is mainly to support the private sector and regulate the markets in order to maintain conditions of macroeconomic stability and a favourable business climate, via the creation of the necessary legal and institutional framework and secure conditions of fair competition.

During the last years, Cyprus has exhibited rising living standards, as shown by the high level of real convergence with the EU. The per capita GDP stood at around 95.8% of the average for the EU27 in 2008,

A beach in Limassol.

driven by the real GDP growth of 3.6% in 2008. However, the international economic crisis, which has deepened intensely since September 2008, has had a major impact on world growth and on the EU. Cyprus has, by 2010, weathered the storm reasonably well compared to other European economies. This can be partly explained by the strong and healthy banking system of Cyprus, which had very limited exposure to toxic products.

> The Central Bank of Cyprus has become part of the European System of Central Banks (ESCB), which, together with the European Central Bank (ECB), conducts monetary policy for the whole Eurozone, based on conditions prevailing in this region.

The crisis primarily affected the construction, real estate and tourism sectors of Cyprus. Given the deceleration of the economy, the government adopted a number of fiscal measures to support the real economy in line with the wider European effort for economic recovery. The measures are targeted towards the tourism and construction sector, which are the areas hit the hardest.

The global economic crisis has also affected the labour market in Cyprus. The unemployment rate reached around 5.3% in 2009, compared to 3.7% in 2008. The "Prevention–Action Plan" promoted in response to the crisis, primarily focused on labour market measures.

Over the last years, public finances have been improved, reaching a surplus of 0.9% of GDP in 2008. However, public finances deteriorated markedly in 2009, and the reason for this being the temporary fiscal stimulus measures adopted by the government to mitigate the negative impact of the crisis on the Cyprus economy and the significant deceleration of the economy.

The Bank of Cyprus headquarters, Nicosia.

KEY POLICY OBJECTIVES

The overriding objective of the economic policy of the government is to enhance long-term growth and the standard of living of all citizens, maintain macroeconomic stability, implement structural reforms which improve the functioning of the market mechanism and ensure that the government sector provides services to the public adequately and efficiently.

MONETARY AND EXCHANGE RATE POLICY

The accession of Cyprus to the Eurozone in January 2008 had the immediate result of losing its monetary policy autonomy. The Central Bank of Cyprus has become part of the European System of Central Banks (ESCB), which, together with the European Central Bank (ECB), conducts monetary policy for the whole Euro- zone, based on conditions prevailing in this region.

FISCAL POLICY

Fiscal policy is geared towards consolidating public finances, with a view to reducing further public debt and thus addressing the long-term sustainability of public finances. Particular emphasis is placed on the need to curtail current expenditure and restructure public spending, in favour of capital expenditure, research and education, which can boost the economy's growth potential. Emphasis is also attached to targeted social spending. The fiscal policy is based on four key pillars:

> The promotion of further structural reforms will enable Cyprus to develop a robust and flexible economy, exhibiting the desired resilience to external shocks.

- The implementation of a Medium-Term Budgetary Framework (MTBF), which will institutionalise expenditure rules, give more independence to spending ministries and, at the same time, increase their accountability for achieving important quantifiable targets.
- The reform of the social welfare system in favour of those who are in greater need.
- The modernisation of the public sector, which will result in leaner and more productive public services.
- The improvement of tax collection, within the present system, by focusing on tackling tax evasion and improving tax administration.

STRUCTURAL REFORMS

The promotion of further structural reforms will enable Cyprus to develop a robust and flexible economy, exhibiting the desired resilience to external shocks, while enhancing the efficiency of the market mechanism and raising the production potential of

The desalination plant in Dhekelia.

the economy. The programme of structural reforms aims at boosting productivity and competitiveness that will deliver high growth and living standards for the citizens of Cyprus. Ongoing reforms include:

- In the labour market, aiming at boosting the supply of labour among females and addressing the high gender pay gap, increasing employability and labour force adaptability particularly through lifelong learning and raising the employment level. The enhancement of physical and human capital is also a key factor in increasing productivity and boosting the economy's potential growth since the development of human capital is especially important in an economy, dominated by the services sector.
- Reforms aimed at strengthening competition, especially in the professional services sector, improving the overall business climate, streamlining the regulatory framework and cutting red tape.

*An interior view of
the Larnaka Airport.*

- Reform of the social security and of the healthcare provision systems which are crucial for tackling the long-term sustainability of public finances.
- Implementation of policies aimed at upgrading the physical infrastructure and improving the functioning of network industries will be intensified, taking into account environmental concerns.

CHALLENGES

A number of challenges must be addressed in the coming years, such as the improvement of productivity which, so far, has not been impressive. In addition, the heavy administrative burden of regulations must be reduced, the use of modern technology and equipment must be further encouraged and more resources must be devoted to research, development and innovation.

The projected demographic changes, with the old-age dependency ratio doubling over the coming decades in the EU and Cyprus, have led to growing concerns regarding the long-term sustainability of the public finances.

Cyprus also faces a major challenge of achieving short-term fiscal consolidation (given the deterioration of the public finances due to the global economic crisis) and long-term sustainability, in view of the budgetary impact of an ageing population. The projected demographic changes, with the old-age dependency ratio doubling over the coming decades in the EU and Cyprus, have led to growing concerns regarding the long-term sustainability of the public finances. Moreover, as a result of the global economic crisis, Cyprus faces a number of challenges in the tourism and construction sector, given that these areas depend to a large extent on foreign demand.

The Larnaka International Airport Terminal.

THE TOURIST INDUSTRY
The Cyprus Tourism Organisation

The foundations of tourism in Cyprus were laid in the early sixties. The industry experienced rapid growth, which was interrupted by the Turkish invasion in the summer of 1974. At that time, all economic activity came to a standstill and the tourist sector suffered a devastating blow when the two highly developed regions of Ammohostos and Kerynia came under the control of the Turkish troops. This resulted in the loss of 13.000 beds constituting 71,7% of the total bed capacity at the time, plus 5.000 beds under construction and about 40% of the island's tourist facilities in restaurants, cafes, bars and nightclubs.

> The liberalisation of the skies has facilitated air travel between Cyprus and EU countries, and the introduction of the euro has made life simpler for tourists visiting Cyprus.

The destruction of the economy called for drastic measures, which would enable its quick reconstruction. Hence, the government recognised that one of the most important measures to be taken concerned the reconstruction of the tourist industry. This task would be achieved through the Cyprus Tourism Organisation (CTO), a semi-government organisation which comes under the Ministry of Commerce, Industry and Tourism, and which is responsible for the planning, promotion and marketing of tourism and the regulation and supervision of all the tourist enterprises of Cyprus.

The Cyprus Tourism Organisation was quick to respond to that challenge and led the reconstruction effort, which was materialised through the support that the private sector received by the government through various policy measures and the entrepreneurial spirit of the Cypriot tourist professionals. Soon enough, Cyprus got back on the global tourist map, and tourism became the backbone of the economy and the main driving force behind the recovery of the Cypriot economy.

TOURISM FOLLOWING EU ACCESSION
The admission of Cyprus as a full EU member-state has generated multifaceted opportunities for the tourist industry of the country.

Beyond the possibilities available for securing funding and financial support for tourist-related projects, Cyprus is afforded the opportunity to voice its opinion on the formulation of policies concerning tourism in Europe, most importantly through its participation in the Tourism Advisory Committee of the EU. The participation of private and public sector in European Union programmes enables them to get acquainted with the functioning of various instruments and institutions of the EU and allows for the sharing of knowledge and exchange of ideas and best practices, thus leading to the adoption of new tools and approaches to be used towards the improvement of the tourist product.

The liberalisation of the skies has facilitated air travel between Cyprus and EU countries, and the introduction of the euro has made life simpler for tourists visiting Cyprus.

Cyprus also benefited from the economic and social cohesion policies of the EU. These EU structural funds (from the European Regional Development Fund and Agricultural Fund) are targeted at the tourist development of the rural areas of Cyprus. As such, they assist the inhabitants of these areas to receive a share of the benefits associated with tourist activity.

A beach in the Protaras area.

Additionaly, local authorities and private sector entities participated in tourism projects under the Community Initiative Interreg. Five such Programmes of interregional co-operation have been completed within the framework of the Interreg IIIA Greece – Cyprus.

As far as the New Programming Period 2007-2013 is concerned, the support of both the European Regional Development Fund and the Agricultural Fund will enable the implementation of a second phase of the actions undertaken during the previous Programming Period, as well as new thematic tourism projects.

In 2009 over 2,1 million tourists visited Cyprus, and generated 1.493,2 million euro compared to 25.700 tourist arrivals in 1960 with C£1,8 million (EUR 3,8 million) in foreign exchange earnings.

CONTRIBUTION TO THE ECONOMY

Contribution of tourism to the economy is of vital importance. In 2009 over 2,1 million tourists visited Cyprus, and generated 1.493,2 million euro compared to 25.700 tourist arrivals in 1960 with C£1,8 million (EUR 3,8 million) in foreign exchange earnings. Tourists are mainly from the UK (49,9%), Scandinavian countries (10,8%), Russia (6,9%), Germany (6,1%), Greece (6,2%) and France (1,2%). Plans in the tourist sector include the construction of new marinas, theme parks and football stadiums and the upgrading of the port of Larnaka. The island's two new modern international airports at Larnaka and Pafos were completed in November 2009 and November 2008 respectively.

ACCOMMODATION

Cyprus offers a wide variety of holiday accommodation ranging from modern, large and luxurious establishments to small and simple family-run operations. Holiday accommodation includes hotels, hotel apartments, tourist villages, tourist villas, camping sites, traditional houses, tourist apartments, furnished apartments, guesthouses and hotels without star. Accommodation in private houses is not available in Cyprus.

The modern tourist accommodation infrastructure in Cyprus is widely recognised as being one of the strengths of the Cyprus tourist product, mainly due to strict legislation governing the establishment and operation of hotels, which demands high standards in accommodation facilities. Despite the above, there is a Strategic Plan which aims at further raising the quality levels of tourist accommodation in Cyprus. English is spoken in all hotels; French and German are also widely spoken.

AGROTOURISM (RURAL CYPRUS)

The implementation of the programme for the development of agrotourism in Cyprus involved the encouragement of the locals - through a number of incentive schemes - to invest in the creation of accommodation and other tourist infrastructure in the countryside by restoring traditional buildings and converting them for tourist use. The availability of the appropriate infrastructure would enable the tourist to holiday in the Cyprus countryside, and get acquainted with its natural and built environment, and the traditions and customs of its people.

As a result of the incentive schemes, 104 traditional houses in 47 villages, with a total capacity of more than 800 beds, have already been converted into

The village
of Kakopetria.

accommodation establishments in accordance with the relevant regulations and have received their classification and operation licence from the CTO. Moreover, a new financial assistance scheme co-funded by EU funds and national funds, has been contributing towards the enhancement of the accommodation product with additional tourist infrastructure (such as handicraft and folk art centres, museums and small wineries), so as make available the integrated rural tourism product to the guests.

NATURE TRAILS

Cyprus offers a network of 72 nature trails, which covers more than a total of 322km. These trails are located in areas of natural beauty such as the Troodos Mountains, the Pafos and Adelphi forests, the Cape Greko and Athalassa national forest parks, the Pitsilia area and the Marathasa Valley.

> In order to encourage further development of golf courses, the government has adopted a golf policy which encourages the development of up to 14 golf courses.

Trails have been sign-posted so as to supply information on the local flora, fauna and geology. Several thematic trails were opened up in recent years. These trails cover themes such as medieval bridges in the Pafos Forest, centenarian trees, traditional activities in villages of the hinterland and waterfalls.

SPORTS TOURISM

This sector is one of the biggest and fastest growing in the global tourist industry. Given the ideal conditions for its development in Cyprus (such as the fine weather, the availability of modern tourist infrastructure, the short distances between the cities, the beach and natural environment and the gradual

upgrading of existing sports infrastructure), the CTO identified sports tourism as one of the special interest products Cyprus should invest in.

GOLF

At present there are three 18-hole international standard golf courses in the Pafos district, while a fourth one is under construction in the same area.

In order to encourage further development of golf courses, the government has adopted a golf policy which encourages the development of up to 14 golf courses. As a result, the private sector has expressed keen interest to develop golf courses in various parts of the island.

A golf course in the Pafos area.

CYCLING

Cyprus has become a destination for cycling enthusiasts both as a place to enjoy the sport through training and competitions and a pleasant means to explore the island. The mild weather conditions, the short distances and rapid changes of terrain entail a variety of different road surfaces and altitude which make Cyprus a paradise for cyclists.

An innovative project is the construction of the first cycling route network in the Troodos area (total length 57 km) within the framework of a project with 50% funding by the EU Structural Funds. The Troodos Cycling Network is the first phase of a broader cycling network that has been designed and will gradually be extended to cover other areas as well.

Cyprus is also part of the Mediterranean Route within the Eurovelo Cycling Network and has established close cooperation with the European Cycling Federation as an associate partner.

> Taking advantage of the strategic geographical position of Cyprus in the Eastern Mediterranean, the Tourism Organisation contributed to the promotion of cruises to and from Cyprus, thereby differentiating and further enriching the Cyprus tourist product.

NAUTICAL TOURISM

Due to the increased demand for berthing spaces and the bright prospects of nautical tourism, the Organisation is implementing, on a step-by-step basis, the masterplan for the development and construction of yacht shelters all along the coastline of Cyprus.

Currently, two marinas are in operation. The development of four new marinas is underway, in Limassol, Agia Napa, Pafos and Larnaka. Most advanced of the four is the project in the Limassol Marina, which is expected to be completed by 2012.

Improvement and extension works are also being carried out in various fishing shelters and small ports along the coast of Cyprus, while the construction of spaces allowing short term berthing of private vessels is under way.

CRUISES

Cruises are a new, alternative form of vacations, and the ever growing demand for cruises worldwide is mostly due to the luxurious product offered to the consumer, who can enjoy care-free vacations.

Taking advantage of the strategic geographical position of Cyprus in the Eastern Mediterranean, the Tourism Organisation contributed to the promotion of cruises to and from Cyprus, thereby differentiating and further enriching the Cyprus tourist product. Cruises offer the tourist the opportunity for short breaks (up to five days) to neighbouring destinations such as Israel, Egypt, Lebanon, Syria, Rhodes and the rest of the Greek islands.

THE EUROPEAN BLUE FLAG CAMPAIGN

The «Blue Flag» is an exclusive eco-label awarded to more than 3.300 beaches and marinas across Europe, Morocco, South Africa, Canada, the Caribbean and New Zealand.

The Blue Flag Campaign, which was launched in 1987 during the European Year for the Environment, is owned and run by the independent non-profit organisation Foundation for Environmental Education (FEE).

The Larnaka Marina.

A cruise ship
in Limassol.

The Blue Flag is geared towards the sustainable development of beaches / marinas through strict criteria dealing with water quality, environmental education and information, environmental management and safety and other services. Being a symbol of environmental quality, it serves as an incentive for local authorities and the private sector to take measures for the overall improvement of the coastal areas in accordance with the above criteria.

Cyprus, as a Mediterranean tourism destination, has recognised the importance of this campaign as one way in which tourism can be better integrated with the coastal environment. At the initiative of the Cyprus Tourism Organisation and with the co-operation of the Cyprus Marine Environment Protection Agency (CYMEPA), the local authorities and the relevant government bodies, Cyprus has introduced the European Blue Flag Campaign and become a full member of FEE in 1995.

The 1995 Pilot Project of the European Blue Flag Campaign, which was jointly undertaken by CYMEPA and the CTO, has successfully established the scheme in Cyprus.

The 1995 Pilot Project of the European Blue Flag Campaign, which was jointly undertaken by CYMEPA and the CTO, has successfully established the scheme in Cyprus. As a result, 54 beaches have been awarded the Blue Flag (the award-winning beaches are featured on the websites www.blueflag.org and www.visitcyprus.com).

The Protaras resort area.

177

A model of the new Limassol Marina to be completed in 2012.

RELIGIOUS TOURISM

The Tourism Organisation places special emphasis on the development of religious tourism in Cyprus due the rich religious history and the religious traditions of the island. The CTO participated as a final beneficiary in an EU Programme within the framework of the European Regional Development Fund, which resulted in the design of thematic religious routes, presented in a guide which has been published in Greek, English and Russian and is available free of charge from CTO.

> The accommodation product of the country features numerous luxury hotels which incorporate excellent conference facilities, and a modern and sophisticated communications infrastructure is in place.

WINE ROUTES

The above is a project co-funded by the European Regional Development Fund, promoting the wine-producing history of Cyprus, its contemporary wine industry and its promising future prospects. Within the framework of this project, six wine routes were identified and developed and have been sign-posted.

Wine tasting.

TEXTILE ROUTE

The "Cyprus Textile Route" is part of a broad European project, which supports cultural co-operation through the online presentation of sites related to textiles. The "European Textiles Routes" project is developed by the European Textiles Network (ETN) and its affiliates. It comprises 29 routes with over 500 stations in 21 countries.

CONFERENCE AND INCENTIVE TOURISM

Cyprus is not only a favourite holiday destination but also a thriving business centre. The accommodation

The ancient city of Amathus, Limassol District.

product of the country features numerous luxury hotels which incorporate excellent conference facilities, and a modern and sophisticated communications infrastructure is in place. Such preconditions pinpoint the great potential of Cyprus to develop into a successful conference and incentive tourism destination.

The Kykkos monastery in the Troodos mountains.

TRADE

The trade sector contributes considerably to the economic growth of the island. Due to its small domestic market and the open nature of its economy, access to international markets is of utmost importance. Because of its location, Cyprus has always had strong economic ties with other countries.

As a result, trade has always played a crucial role in the development of the economy. Cyprus' accession to the EU represents a turning point which has affected Cyprus' international trade, fostering exports as a driving force in the economy. This was developed even further with Cyprus' adoption of the euro on 1 January 2008. With regard to the commodity structure of Cyprus exports, manufactured products account for 58,1%, agricultural products (raw) for 21,34% and processed agricultural products for 14,86%. The European Union is Cyprus' most important trading partner. In 2009, domestic exports to the EU reached around 51,7% of domestic exports, mainly to the UK (8,5%), Greece (22,1%) and Germany (8,3%). In addition, 14,1% of total exports went to Near and Middle Eastern countries, whereas 6% to other Asian countries.

> The main products re-exported from Cyprus are tobacco, processed foodstuffs, beverages, textiles and textile articles, minerals and chemicals.

The main products re-exported from Cyprus in 2009 were tobacco, processed foodstuffs, beverages, textiles and textile articles, minerals and chemicals. Improvements in port infrastructure and equipment include advancements in operational methods and

information systems used for the handling of vessels and cargo. Furthermore, Cyprus has a thriving ship management system.

RE-EXPORTS

Transit cargo enjoys special treatment at the Cyprus ports. Indicative of the position of Cyprus as a main transhipment centre is the substantial amount of

A Nicosia-Limassol motorway interjunction.

products re-exported, which reached EUR 643 million in 2008. The bulk of these re-exports, about 51%, was directed mainly towards the countries of the European Union. They were followed by Near and Middle Eastern countries which absorbed 12%, while 2,5% were directed to other European countries. Asian and North America also absorb about 1% and 0,5% respectively.

EXPORTS OF SERVICES

Cyprus is also an exporter of services. The services sector dominates economic activity in Cyprus as indicated by its 80% contribution to GVA (Gross Value Added). Over the last years, Cyprus has undertaken a major role in facilitating the provision of services and support to business people and professionals worldwide.

The Trade Centres are actively involved in the promotion of Cyprus as an international business centre, as well as in the attraction of foreign investments.

Services include banking and financial services, insurance, advertising, legal, architecture and civil engineering, accounting and auditing, consultancy, design, electrical and mechanical engineering, market research, medical, printing and publishing, public relations, education, software development, tourism and related services.

PROMOTION OF EXPORTS

The main objective of the Ministry of Commerce, Industry and Tourism regarding the area of trade is the expansion of exports of goods and services. In order to achieve its goal the Ministry has developed and put into effect a plan of action. This plan is designed in such a way as to improve the ability of the Cypriot enterprises to penetrate into foreign markets.

This plan of actions involves much more than advertising and includes amongst others, the introduction of export oriented schemes, the participation in international trade fairs, the organisation of business missions and seminars abroad, public relations and market research.

The Ministry operates also eleven Trade Centres, situated in carefully targeted markets. At present, the Ministry maintains centres in Austria, Egypt, EU, France, Germany, Greece, Lebanon, Poland, Russian Federation, the United Arab Emirates, the United Kingdom, and the U.S.A. The sole responsibility of the Trade Centres is the promotion of exports of goods and services in overseas markets. Furthermore, the Trade Centres are actively involved in the promotion of Cyprus as an international business centre, as well as in the attraction of foreign investments.

IMPORTS

Imports of consumer goods and intermediate inputs (raw materials) make up for most of the total imports, accounting for almost 30%. These are followed by fuels and lubricants (17%), transport equipment (16%), and capital goods (9%). In 2009, the European Union (EU27) remained the main source of supply of goods to Cyprus, with a share of 71,5% of total imports/arrivals. Major suppliers within the Union were Greece (19,9%), Italy (10,8%), the United Kingdom (9,3%), Germany (8,9%) and France (3,8%).

Imports from Israel, China, Brazil and Japan accounted for 6,9% , 5,4%, 0,2% and 2% respectively.

The Marfin Laiki Bank
headquarters, Nicosia.

MANUFACTURING AND INDUSTRY

Manufacturing in 2009 is estimated to have accounted for 7,5% of GVA and provides employment to 9,7% of the workforce. The main industries are food, beverages, tobacco, textiles, clothing, footwear, leather goods, metal products, chemicals and plastic products.

The contribution of the manufacturing sector to GDP has exhibited a downward trend since the early 1980s. This sector is characterised by problems of competitiveness, due, inter alia, to the small size of the majority of manufacturing units, which negatively affect their capacity to utilise advanced technology and modern methods of management, production and marketing. Other problems lie in the structural weakness of the sector, the rising labour costs and low productivity. There is also international competition on the one hand from the high-wage producers, who have combined design, quality and new forms of flexible production, and on the other from the low-wage mass producers of China and South-East Asia.

> There are currently about 600 industrial enterprise units operating in the Industrial Estates and engaged in a wide spectrum of activities.

Faced with this situation the government has reformulated its policy to facilitate technological upgrading of the industry. More specifically, the government has set the following priorities.
- To attract and develop high-tech industry
- To assist in the reconstruction of existing industries
- To improve productivity
- To attract foreign investment.

Celebrations marking Cyprus' admission into the Eurozone.

Foreign capital can play a major role in these efforts as it contributes substantially to the production of high technology and expertise. Additionally, Cyprus' membership in the European Union makes it possible for small and medium enterprises to participate in the various programmes concerning industrial technology, professional training and product development in this way assisting the process of restructuring.

A mobile desalination plant in Moni.

INDUSTRIAL ESTATES AND FREE ZONES

The government has established twelve Industrial Estates across the island and one Free Zone. There are currently about 600 industrial enterprise units operating in the Industrial Estates and engaged in a wide spectrum of activities. The government has allocated to these industrial enterprises appropriate land, varying in size according to the needs of each unit, on a long-term lease base. The yearly lease rental depends on the location of the industrial estate.

> The government of Cyprus has made efforts to create a regulatory climate conducive to investment, innovation and entrepreneurship, to lower costs of doing business and to remove unnecessary procedures.

The Free Zone in Cyprus is situated in the Larnaka area near the airport and has been operating since 1980. The objectives of the establishment of the Free Zone are the following:

- the attraction of foreign investments
- the creation of employment opportunities
- theincrease of exports and the inflow of foreign currency
- the utilisation of the geographical position of Cyprus, as well as the advanced infrastructure.

Any person can apply to the Ministry of Commerce, Industry & Tourism to obtain a licence for establishing an industrial unit within the Larnaka Free Zone for operating trade work or manufacturing.

SMALL AND MEDIUM-SIZED ENTERPRISES

The economy of Cyprus is dominated by small and medium-sized enterprises (SMEs). Almost all enterprises (99,9%) employ less than 250 persons whereas the overwhelming majority (95%) employs less than 10 persons. The total number of SME's in Cyprus is 61.041. The government of Cyprus has made efforts to create a regulatory climate conducive to investment, innovation and entrepreneurship, to lower costs of doing business and to remove unnecessary procedures which act as a barrier against the development of SME's in Cyprus.

The Dhekelia power station.

EMS DATAPOST

The Department of Postal Services.

AGRICULTURE

Agriculture continues to be a vital sector of the economy of Cyprus, despite its gradual decrease due to the development of other sectors such as tourism and services, and the difficulties which have emerged as a result of the intensive competitive environment. Nowadays, the importance of agriculture is not only defined by financial indicators but also by the fact that it has a multi-functional role. In addition to the production of food, it contributes significantly to the preservation of the environment and provides the means for improving and protecting life in the countryside.

During the period 1960-1974, the agricultural sector expanded rapidly, but in 1974 it was severely affected by the Turkish invasion, which resulted in the occupation of 36,2% of Cyprus. More specifically, the Turkish forces occupied an area, which accounted for 46% of crop production and much higher percentages of citrus (79%), cereals (68%), tobacco (100%), carobs (86%) and green fodders (65%), while 45% of livestock production was from this area.

The value of imported industrial products of agricultural origin was €306,8 million, making up 5,2% of total imports for home consumption.

Despite the obligatory concentration of the population in the less productive part of the island, it was possible through concerted efforts and heavy investment in land improvement and irrigation to reactivate the agricultural sector and to reach the pre-1974 production levels.

CONTRIBUTION OF AGRICULTURE TO GDP AND EMPLOYMENT

Agriculture and Fishing contributed 1,9% to GVA in 2009 and provided employment to 7% of the

working population. Principal crops are potatoes, other vegetables, cereals, citrus, grapes and olives. Livestock farming is mainly in cattle, sheep, goats, pigs and poultry. Fish production is derived from inshore and trawl fishing and marine agriculture.

AGRICULTURAL TRADE

Agricultural exports constituted around 17,3% or €82,7million of total domestic exports in 2009 whereas imports of raw agricultural products reached €163 million. The value of imported capital goods for agriculture accounted for €33,9mn in 2009 and €37,2mn in 2008. The main agricultural commodities imported include cereals, meat and milk products, and processed food items.

In 2009, EU countries absorbed 73% of raw agricultural products and 62,5% of industrial products of agricultural origin. Cyprus imported agricultural products from EU member countries at a value of €383,9 million, 63,4% of which were industrial products of agricultural origin. The value of imported industrial products of agricultural origin was €306,8

The Pissouri bay.

million, making up 5,2% of total imports for home consumption.

The total agriculture output in 2009 was €677,2 million, 42,93% of which represented the value of crop production, 49,97% the value of livestock production and 6% the value of forest and other products.

THE STRUCTURE OF AGRICULTURE
The total value of crop production increased to €290,7 million in 2009 compared to €669,1 million in 2008. Cereal production as the main rain fed crop of the country, continued dropping and reached 32,7 thousand tons from 6,3 thousand tons in 2008. This is attributed to the unfavourable weather conditions.

The livestock sub-sector contributes to about 47% of the agricultural gross output and comprises dairy cattle, sheep and goats, swine and poultry.

Potato production increased to 131,8 thousand tons in 2009 compared to 115 thousand tons in 2008. The total citrus fruit production (oranges, lemons, mandarins and grapefruit) remained at approximately the same levels of 2008 (116,4 thousand tons in 2009 and 111,8 thousand tons in 2008).

LIVESTOCK
The livestock sub-sector contributes to about 47% of the agricultural gross output and comprises dairy cattle, sheep and goats, swine and poultry. The total value of livestock production in 2009 was €338,4 million of which 65% represented the value of meat production, 28% the value of milk and 7% the value of eggs and other livestock products. Dairy cattle, swine and poultry

are concentrated in relatively large commercial units around urban centres, while sheep and goat farms are scattered throughout the country, operating under semi-intensive or free large management. The development of livestock production has been given great attention both quantitatively and qualitatively.

agriculture

WATER MANAGEMENT

Throughout its long history Cyprus has always been confronted with the problem of water shortage. Having no rivers with perennial flow and with a highly variable precipitation, the country experiences frequent droughts. The mean annual precipitation, including snowfall, amounts to approximately 500mm, whereas during the past years this amount fell to 461mm.

Up until 1970, groundwater was the main source of water for both domestic supply and irrigation. As a result, almost all aquifers were seriously depleted because of over-pumping, and seawater intrusion was observed in most of the coastal aquifers. At the time large quantities of surface water were lost through run-offs.

The water problem and its exacerbation over the years, were recognised early enough by the relevant state authorities, which, aided by international organisations, established a long-term programme to combat the problem effectively.

After independence, attention was turned to the systematic study and construction of water development works, both for storage and recharge purposes, followed by the implementation of a long-term plan for the construction of major development projects, which involved the building of a large number of dams.

Today, the total storage capacity of the dams is about 327,5 million cubic metres (MCM) of water, compared to 6 MCM in 1960, a performance which is really impressive when compared to other countries of the same size and development level.

Despite the remarkable progress in the sector, quantities of water available for human consumption and irrigation were not adequate. This was due to an increased demand for water, declining precipitation, global climate changes and the greenhouse phenomenon.

To remedy the situation, desalination units were constructed aiming at providing water supply for the major residential and tourist centres independent of rainfall.

The desalination plant in Dhekelia.

The Farmakas Dam.

193

MARINE RESOURCES

Cyprus has developed activities in multidisciplinary field of activities such as the sustainable use of marine resources, the development and proper management of aquaculture, marine ecology, the protection of endangered species and habitats, the physical and chemical oceanography and the prevention and combatting of marine pollution.

Furthermore, a Fishing Vessel Register has been set up in which all fishing vessels are registered so that there is a record of the fishing capacity of the Cyprus Fishing Fleet. This data is communicated to the E-Commission every three months.

The annual production of fish is about 5.569 tons valued at €74,1 million. Fish production is mainly derived from inshore fishery, trawl fishery, territorial and international waters and purse seiners as well as from aquaculture. The Cyprus Fishing Fleet consists of 498 small fishing boats, 12 trawlers and 30 multipurpose vessels fishing swordfish and tunas.

> Fish production is mainly derived from inshore fishery, trawl fishery, territorial and international waters and purse seiners as well as from aquaculture.

Currently, there are three marine fish hatcheries and one shrimp hatchery/ farm on land, seven private offshore cage farms producing mainly sea bass and sea bream and three offshore cage farms producing blue fin tuna. Additionally, there were in operation seven small trout farms, producing mainly rainbow trout and two farms culturing ornamental fish. There are also ten fishing shelters in operation.

A decision has also been taken for the construction of an auction centre which is essential since Cyprus has joined the European Union. The auction centre will include inland installations for the trading of fishing products as well as a port for fishing vessels.

Moreover, great importance is given to the protection of the marine biodiversity, endangered species and habitats, as well as the establishment of marine protected areas within the Natura 2000 network. Currently, there is only one coastal/marine protected area, the Lara-Toxeftra marine reserve, which was established in 1989 under the provisions of the Fisheries Law and Regulations, for the protection of nesting habitats of the marine turtles, Chelonia mydas and Caretta caretta.

A fishing shelter
in Protaras.

195

MERCHANT SHIPPING

The Cyprus Register of Ships has shown phenomenal growth in the last twenty-five years. In the early eighties Cyprus ranked thirty-second on the list of leading maritime nations. It now ranks in tonnage terms as one of the ten largest in the world with a merchant fleet exceeding 20 million gross tons. Also, the Cypriot merchant fleet ranks third in the European Union with a percentage of above 12% of the total fleet of the 27 EU member states.

> Cyprus also contributes significantly to the achievement of the objective of the IMO, namely safer seas and cleaner oceans.

Cyprus is considered as one of the leading third-party ship management centres in the world. More than sixty ship management companies are established and operate in Cyprus, many of which are considered among the largest ship management companies in the world. In conjunction with these more than one hundred companies have been established with shipping related activities, ranging from marine insurance, ship chartering, ship-broking, financial services, equipment suppliers and telecommunications, to port services, transhipment operations, shipping agents, ship chandlers and ship bunkering.

The above achievements can be partly attributed to the introduction by the government of new legislation containing especially favourable provisions for ship-owning and ship management companies. This legislation introduced the tonnage tax instead of income tax as well as the elimination of tax on dividends received from a ship-owning company, on capital gains, on the sale or transfer of a Cypriot vessel or the shares of a ship owning company.

As regards the further development of Cyprus merchant shipping and the enhancement of its international reputation as a maritime flag, the government has concluded cooperation agreements on merchant shipping with several other countries. It also participates as a full member in the activities of all international organisations, which are involved in the area of shipping. Cyprus has ratified all international maritime conventions, which are currently in force.

The efforts to improve the image of shipping are not limited to Cyprus shipping. As a member of the IMO Council, Cyprus plays a significant role in the formulation of the future strategy and the regulatory work of the Organisation and is influential in the decision making process. Cyprus also contributes significantly to the achievement of the objective of the IMO, namely safer seas and cleaner oceans.

The port of Limassol.

MARITIME SAFETY AND SECURITY

During the last few years, Cyprus has adopted a series of measures aiming at the upgrading and the modernisation of Cyprus Shipping through a safety policy which focused on the effective control of the ships and the improvement of the quality of their fleet.

Particular attention has also been given to the qualifications of the seafarers employed on Cyprus ships as well as to their living and working conditions.

This policy proved to be quite successful and is evidenced by the fact that Cyprus is now permanently on the "White list" of both the Paris and the Tokyo MOU, on port state control. Furthermore, the safety record of the flag has been improved; the number of serious accidents and the loss of lives have been reduced over the years.

The activities of the Ports Authority are two-fold. On the one hand, it is responsible for the administration, construction and management of the port infrastructure and on the other, it carries out activities related to the provision, coordination and control of port services offered.

CONTRIBUTION TO ECONOMY

The contribution of merchant shipping to the economy of Cyprus is significant. The Cyprus government is well aware that through shipping, Cyprus has distinguished itself by achieving remarkable international ranking and recognition far beyond its size and boundaries.

Shipping contributes approximately 2% of the Gross Domestic Product of Cyprus. 3.500 persons are employment in shipping activities the majority of whom are Cypriots.

PORTS AUTHORITY

All ports facilities of the island are under the jurisdiction of the Cyprus Ports Authority (CPA), a statutory

The port of Limassol.

body set up in 1973. It is the main investor in Cyprus ports, though a significant share of remunerative port activities are carried out by the private sector, as for example the horizontal transportation of cargo within the port and stevedore activities.

The activities of the Authority are two-fold. On the one hand, it is responsible for the administration, construction and management of the port infrastructure and on the other, it carries out activities related to the provision, coordination and control of port services offered.

Cyprus benefits from being strategically positioned at the crossroads of three continents (Europe, Asia and Africa). As a result of this, the CPA aims to attract movement of transit trade and cruise ships while at the same time providing high standard commercial services at the lowest possible cost. In keeping with this strategy, the CPA aims to evolve to a landlord of ports and regulator of port services, in line with the general policy that is being followed within the European Union.

The port of Pafos.

Cyprus is connected to a significant number of overseas ports and is included in the itineraries of more than fifty international shipping lines. Approximately 5.000 ships call at Cypriot ports and terminals annually. Of these 67% are cargo ships, and 8% passenger ships. The main categories of ships calling at Cypriot ports are in order of frequency: tankers (20%), container ships (19%), conventional (15%), ro-ro type ships (13%) and passenger ships (8%).

PASSENGER TRAFFIC
Cyprus has established itself as one of the most important cruise centres in the Eastern Mediterranean and it is included in the itineraries of most of the Mediterranean as well as the international cruise ships which sail in the region. Around 32 international cruise ships included Cyprus in their Mediterranean itineraries, carrying out 181 calls and transporting some 231.000 passengers. Moreover, Cyprus is a permanent base for cruise ships which carry out excursions in the region on a regular basis.

> Around 32 international cruise ships included Cyprus in their Mediterranean itineraries, carrying out 181 calls and transporting some 231.000 passengers.

Sea-borne traffic is serviced by a modern and highly integrated national port system, composed of the multipurpose ports of Limassol and Larnaka, the industrial port of Vassiliko and four specialised oil terminals at Larnaka, Dekeleia, Moni and Vassiliko.

PORTS
The port of Limassol is the main commercial port of Cyprus and serves the country's overseas trade and sea-borne passenger traffic and acts as a transhipment centre for the region. With a quay length of 2,030 metres the CPA has proceeded with the dredging of the western container terminal basin to sixteen meters and the turning circle and entrance channel to seventeen metres. Additionally, it has been decided to expand the quay of the western basin by 500 meters and construction works are expected to be completed by the end of 2011. Preliminary designs have also been made for the construction of a new passenger terminal which will meet the criteria set by the Schengen Convention. It is expected that detailed designs will be prepared and the project will be ready in 2011.

The Larnaka port is the second largest port of Cyprus and is situated in the southeastern part of Cyprus. With a quay length of 666 metres and dredged depth to twelve metres, it serves some specialised trade and the commercial needs of Larnaka such as the exports of agricultural products and imports of vegetables and animal feed. However, it is scheduled for redevelopment into a specialised state-of-the-art passenger/leisure port.

The Pafos port is in the south-western part of Cyprus at a central point of the city of Pafos. The port mainly serves small recreational ships and fishing vessels. In addition, the port together with the Pafos Castle, which is located within the port area, give the city a picturesque character.

The port of Vassiliko situated in the southern part of the Cyprus between Limassol and Larnaka, is the main port for handling industrial types of cargo such as dangerous cargo and humid fuels.

The ports of Famagusta, Keryneia, Karavostassi and Xeros are in the area under military occupation by Turkey since 1974, and have therefore been declared by the government closed to shipping and navigation and as prohibited ports of entry and exit.

The port of Limassol.

education

- PRE-PRIMARY EDUCATION
- PRIMARY EDUCATION
- SECONDARY EDUCATION
- HIGHER EDUCATION
- SPORTS

education

As indicated by the high adult literacy rate of 97 percent, education is a top priority for the people and the state of Cyprus. According to the EU Statistical Service, Cyprus ranks second, after Finland, as regards the proportion of the population aged 25-64 with tertiary education. Moreover, after Luxemburg, Cyprus has the second highest percentage of tertiary students studying in another EU country, while it ranks second among the EU countries regarding public expenditure on education as a percentage of GDP.

The Education system in Cyprus consists of the following stages:

PRE-PRIMARY EDUCATION

The Ministry of Education and Culture is responsible for the education of children of the age of three years and over, who study in public, community and private nursery schools.

Emphasis is given on the attribution of personal interest towards each child separately, depending on his peculiarities, skills and needs, on love, support, trust, acceptance, safety and respect of individual diversity, peculiarity and variation.

Pre-Primary Education complements the task of a family, for the support, with every means, of the most complete possible development of a child, for satisfaction of the basic needs of his personality and his exposure to supporting and constructive experiences, with the aim of realising his skills and capabilities and of developing a positive self-image.

The nursery school aims towards a way of life that would retain, as many elements of the natural way of a family life, with emphasis on a free and creative activity of a child, through individual approaches that focus on children, in an environment that reinforces cooperative learning, experimentation and team work. Emphasis is given on the attribution of personal interest towards each child separately, depending on his peculiarities, skills and needs, on love, support, trust, acceptance, safety and respect of individual diversity, peculiarity and variation.

There are public, community and private nursery schools in Cyprus. With the introduction since 2004, of free compulsory pre-primary education one year before admission of a child to a Primary school, all operating expenses of public nursery schools are undertaken by the Ministry of Education and Culture. All children, who reside permanently or temporarily in Cyprus, have the right for registration in a public nursery school.

PRIMARY EDUCATION

Primary education is compulsory and has a duration of six years. The cornerstone of the aims of Primary Education was and continues to be the balanced development of children's personality, with the creation of favourable conditions for the conquest of knowledge, the development of equitable attitudes and the cultivation of skills, rendering them capable of undertaking future responsibilities and action in the continuously changing world.

The main objective of Primary Education is to organise, ensure and offer to all the children, independent of age, sex, intellectual capabilities, family and social background, such teaching opportunities, so that they:

- Develop in a balanced way at the knowledge, emotional and psychokinetic level, taking advantage to the greatest degree possible, the means offered by modern technology.
- Deal successfully with the various problems that they may possibly face as well as any difficulties of adapting to their school and broader environment.
- Gain positive attitudes towards education develop social apprehension, competitiveness, devotion to human values, respect of cultural heritage and human rights, appreciation of beauty and appetite for creativity and love for life and nature, so that they become sensitive over issues of conservation and improvement of the environment.

Both public and private primary schools operate in Cyprus. Depending on the number of schoolteachers in each public school they are distinguished in single, double, triple and multi teaching post schools. In case the number of students in a school is smaller than fifteen arrangements are put in place to merge two or more primary schools and create a bigger regional primary school. In case of a merger of schools, the State subsidizes the transportation of students from other communities to the regional schools.

The concept of all day school operates in certain schools on a voluntary basis, from October to May, with four additional afternoon periods for the children of the fourth, fifth and sixth class, four times a week.

SECONDARY EDUCATION

Secondary General Education offers a six-year programme of education for students aged between 12 and 18. At the Gymnasium (Lower Secondary school) the main orientation is the general humanistic education. Education at the Gymnasium is compulsory for the first three years up to the age of 15.

At the Lyceum the educational system is more flexible and offers various specialisations depending on an inclination, skills and interests of a student. Particularly, following the adoption of the concept of a Unified Lyceum on a nationwide scale, from the school year 2000-2001 onwards, flexibility and prospects opening up for students increased considerably.

The basic aim of the Gymnasium is to promote the development of students in relation to capabilities of their age and corresponding demands of life. The Gymnasium constitutes a self-existent school unit of general educational direction. It complements the general education which primary school provides and prepares students to accept the increased general humanistic education which it provides, preparing them at the same time to attend, afterwards, the Lyceum or the Technical Education, which they can select after their graduation from the Gymnasium.

Within the context of the objectives of the Lyceum students are expected to:

- Form their personality in a harmonious and all-embracing way by developing free, critical thinking, initiative, collectiveness and imagination.

> The basic aim of the Gymnasium is to promote the development of students in relation to capabilities of their age and corresponding demands of life. Gymnasium constitutes a self-existent school unit of general educational direction.

- Develop intellectual, moral, aesthetic and physical characteristics and skills, so that they can face society, science, technology, arts and more general constituents of culture with creativity and an innovative approach.
- Develop the essential abilities, knowledge, skills, attitudes and values that will allow them to continue their study within the frames of lifelong education and training and will facilitate their access to the productive process following additional specialisation or training.
- Finally transform into citizens who will be conscious of the problems faced today by the humanity and be capable to act effectively, in an individual and collective way, while dealing with these problems.

Instead of the Lyceum, pupils may choose to attend Secondary Technical and Vocational Education, which provides them with knowledge and skills that will prepare them to enter the workforce or pursue further studies in their area of interest.

ΓΥΜΝΑΣΙΟ ΡΙΖΟΚΑΡΠΑΣΟΥ

Pupils of the Rizokarpaso Gymnasium, in the Turkish occupied area of Cyprus.

HIGHER EDUCATION

Government policy with regard to higher education aims to fulfill the local needs for higher education and to establish Cyprus as a regional educational and research centre, a hub for international scholars and students alike. The higher education system in Cyprus is shaped by the European Higher Education Area as outlined by the Bologna Process. Higher Education in Cyprus consists of the public and private institutions of Higher Education at the University and non-University level.

STATE UNIVERSITIES

 Πανεπιστήμιο Κύπρου

The University of Cyprus (www.ucy.ac.cy)

The University of Cyprus was founded to satisfy the increasing educational needs of the Cypriot population and to fulfill social, financial and other objectives of the Republic. Scientific research is promoted and funded in all departments with an aim to contribute to academic and scholarly development, and to meet local and international needs and demands. The law, which regulates the establishment and functioning of the University of Cyprus was passed by the House of Representatives in 1989. The University of Cyprus admitted its first students in 1992. Nowadays, it offers programmes of studies in three cycles: «Degree» (first cycle), «Master» (second cycle) and «Doctorate» (third cycle).

The Open University of Cyprus (www.ouc.ac.cy)

The Open University of Cyprus was established by a law adopted by the House of Representatives in 2002, and admitted its first students in September 2006 at two post-graduate programmes of studies by distance learning: «Education Studies» and «Administration of Health Units». Nowadays it offers, in to addition, the undergraduate programme of studies «Studies of Hellenic Civilisation» and the post-graduate programme of studies «Specialisation in Information Systems».

The Cyprus University of Technology (www.cut.ac.cy)

The Cyprus University of Technology was established by a law passed by the House of Representatives in 2003 and admitted its first students in September 2007. The Cyprus University of Technology is a conventional type of a university that offers programmes of studies orientated mainly towards applied sciences.

PRIVATE UNIVERSITIES

The House of Representatives enacted Law 109 (I)/2005 which regulates the establishment and operation of Private Universities in Cyprus. The Law came into force on July 29, 2005. The first private universities in Cyprus commenced their operation following a relevant decision by the Council of Ministers in 2007. Currently, the following private universities operate in Cyprus:

1.**Frederick University (www.frederick.ac.cy)**
2.**European University Cyprus (www.euc.ac.cy)**
3.**The University of Nicosia (www.unic.ac.cy)**
4. **Neapolis University - Pafos (www.nup.ac.cy)**

The Cyprus Forestry College.

STATE TERTIARY EDUCATION INSTITUTIONS

Tertiary education in Cyprus is also offered by a number of State Tertiary Education Institutions, none of which has a university status. Today, the following non-University State Tertiary Education Institutions operate:

- Forestry College of Cyprus
- Higher Hotel Institute
- Mediterranean Institute of Management (MIM)
- Police Academy

PRIVATE TERTIARY EDUCATION INSTITUTIONS

There are currently 25 Private Tertiary Education Institutions (PTEI) in Cyprus, some of which maintain branches in other cities of Cyprus besides Nicosia. Private Tertiary Education Institutions (PTEI) do not enjoy a university status, but they offer both academic and vocational programmes of studies at the undergraduate and post-graduate levels.

The competent authority for quality assurance, evaluation and accreditation of programmes of studies offered by private institutions of tertiary education is the Council of Educational Evaluation-Accreditation (CEEA/S.E.K.A.P.), which is a member of ENQA (the European Association for Quality Assurance in Higher Education). Currently, a large number of programmes offered by private institutions of tertiary education have been subject to educational evaluation and accreditation by S.E.K.A.P. These programmes fall under the following categories:

- Academic and Vocational programmes of studies leading to the award of: Certificate (one year), Diploma (two years) and Higher Diploma (three years). Access to these programmes requires a Leaving Certificate or an equivalent qualification.
- First cycle programmes, lasting for four academic years leading to the award of a degree and a Bachelor's degree. Access to these programmes requires Apolyterion or an equivalent qualification.
- Second cycle programmes, lasting for two academic years of continuous education and leading to the award of a Masters Degree. Admission to these programmes requires a Degree or a Bachelor or an equivalent qualification.

SPORTS

The history of sports in Cyprus goes back many centuries. Inscriptions found in various archaeological sites both on the island and in Greece bear witness to the Cypriots' love for sports and to their success in Pan-Hellenic and Olympic contests of ancient times at Olympia, Pythia, Isthmia and elsewhere.

This is further attested by the ancient stadia of Cyprus at Kourion, Salamis, Pafos, Kition and Lapithos, which existed until the Byzantine Period. Evidence shows that during the Middle Ages athletics remained a favourite Cypriot pastime.

> During the period between 1969 and 1974, efforts were made to organise the Cyprus Sports Organisation, with the basic aim of establishing National Federations and affiliating them to the corresponding World Federations.

The first athletic club was founded in Limassol in 1897. After that similar clubs began to spring up across the island in each of the major towns.

CYPRUS SPORTS ORGANISATION

Cyprus has a long history in athletics with inscriptions recording the participation of Cypriot athletes in the Ancient Olympic Games. When the Olympic Games were revived in 1896, Cyprus participated with athletes competing under the Greek flag.

In 1969 legislation was passed establishing the Cyprus Sports Organisation as a semi-governmental organisation. Its basic aims are the development of out-of-school sports, the coordination of the sports life of the island, the cultivation of the Olympic ideal and the promotion of Cyprus in the field of international sports.

Opening Ceremony of the XIII Games of the Small States of Europe held in Cyprus in June 2009.

During the period between 1969 and 1974, efforts were made to organise the Cyprus Sports Organisation, with the basic aim of establishing National Federations and affiliating them to the corresponding World Federations. However, after 1974 and up to 1980, efforts were devoted to the revitilisation of Cypriot sports in the aftermath of the Turkish invasion and to creating the necessary infrastructure for sports despite the enormous economic and other problems the country was facing.

The years between 1980 until 1990 saw the presence of Cyprus in world sports with its participation in international events, initially with results that were sometimes disappointing but always with the hope of

Municipal Olympic
swimming pool, Larnaka.

something better. The first participation of Cyprus as an independent state was at the Moscow Olympics in 1980. The rapid development of Cypriot sports that followed was unprecedented for Cyprus. It was during this decade that the foundations of the course of development of Cypriot sports were laid. The programme "Sports for All" began operating and was geared to a great extent for children. However, the years that followed up to 2000 were marked by Cyprus' intensified presence at international meetings, with important successes and distinctions. Sports in Cyprus followed the European course and at the same time responded fully to the European conventions and undertakings which the European Sports Charter of Rhodes and the Code of Ethics established. After 2000 there was a steady harmonisation with Europe with the most important goal of the Cyprus Sports Organisation being the gradual and substantial implementation of the resolutions of the Council of Europe and the European Union with the aim of "pure and beneficial sports".

> The first participation of Cyprus as an independent state was at the Moscow Olympics in 1980. The rapid development of Cypriot sports that followed was unprecedented for Cyprus.

CYPRUS OLYMPIC COMMITTEE

The Cyprus Olympic Committee (COC) was established in 1974 and in 1979 it became a full member of the International Olympic Committee. These years have been marked by activities strongly linked to the ideals of the Olympics and also significant achievements, which have merited recognition and appreciation on an international level.

The first time Cyprus participated in international games officially under the auspices of the Cyprus Olympic Committee, was in 1980 in the 13th Winter Olympic Games held at Lake Placid in the United States. Later, in the same year, Cyprus participated in the Summer Olympic Games, which were held in Moscow.

Since then, Cyprus has participated in all the major international events, providing its athletes with access to sporting events such as the Olympic Games, the Commonwealth Games, the Mediterranean Games, the Games of the Small States of Europe and the European Youth Olympic Festival. Even though Cyprus is a small country, Cypriot athletes have won international distinctions which the country is proud of.

The Cyprus Olympic Committee has acquired prestige through its remarkable activities. In 1982, Juan Antonio Samaranch visited Cyprus for the first time in his capacity as President of the International Olympic Committee.

In 1987, the National Olympic Academy was established in Nicosia during a glamorous ceremony. Every year, the Academy organises conferences with speakers and participants from the international world of sports.

In 2009, Cyprus successfully hosted the Games of the Small States of Europe and was atop of the medal board. The Games were so successful that they became a reference point for the European

Opening Ceremony of the XIII Games of the Small States of Europe held in Cyprus in June 2009.

215

Olympic Committees. It is worth mentioning that the Cyprus Olympic Committee played a pioneering role in institutionalising them.

The status of the Cyprus Olympic Committee within the IOC and international sport circles is constantly being upgraded. The COC has signed protocols for co-operation with other countries. It successfully organises two events each year, a seminar on the Union of the European Olympic Committees and the Meeting of the Union's Executive Committee. Members of its Executive Board are elected to important positions in the International Sport Movement.

In 2009, Cyprus successfully hosted the Games of the Small States of Europe and was atop of the medal board. The Games were so successful that they became a reference point for the European Olympic Committees.

THE OLYMPIC HOUSE
In 2006, the Olympic House and Park was inaugurated to house most sports federations. The Olympic House is a major component for sports in Cyprus and an important landmark in the activities of the Cyprus Olympic Committee. It is located in an area of 7.500 square meters, at the entrance to Nicosia. Its architecture expresses three basic dimensions which are the components of the Olympic ideal:

- The Universal Dimension: cultivating and spreading the ancient spirit of the Olympics, in the sphere of co-operation, emulation and peace in the world.
- The Historical Dimension: preserving and reviving a 3000 year-old concept.

XIII Games of the Small States of Europe held in Cyprus in June 2009.

- The Sports Dimension: promoting simultaneous physical and spiritual exercise as an essential human activity.

Hundreds of events (award banquets, seminars and cultural gatherings) have taken place in the CYTA "fair play" room which hosts all the activities that take place in the Olympic House.

Olympic House.

PARTICIPATION IN INTERNATIONAL SPORTS EVENTS

The Cyprus Olympic Committee has shown steady progress over the years in major competitions. It is indicative that in every new major competition its delegation is more successful than in the previous events.

In 2008 the committee's main aim was to show a good performance at the Olympic Games of Beijing. This goal was reached with two athletes in the Men's Skeet reaching the final. Antonis Nicolaides was fourth, missing out on the bronze medal in the shoot off process by one missed clay disc. George Achilleos was right behind him achieving the fifth position. These were the highest positions Cyprus has ever had in an Olympic final as an independent state. In the women's event of skeet shooting Andri Eleftheriou also made the final and reached the seventh position, making her the only Cypriot woman finalist in the Olympics ever.

> In 2008 the committee's main aim was to show a good performance at the Olympic Games of Beijing. This goal was reached with two athletes in the Men's Skeet reaching the final.

In other major competitions, Cypriot athletes have had great results. Kyriakos Ioannou won the Silver medal in High Jump at the IAAF World Championships in Athletics in Berlin in 2009. In 2007 and 2008, Pavlos Kontides was the world junior sailing champion in the laser radial category, and became the only athlete to ever accomplish such a feat. Also, at the 2009 World Juniors Championships Michalis Malekkides won another gold for Cyprus in the RSX windsurfing category. In Gymnastics, Erodotos Giorgallas was fourth at the European championships in the rings

Eleni Artymata at the Olympic Stadium in Berlin in August 2009.

Kyriakos Ioannou wins the Silver medal in High Jump at the IAAF World Championships in Athletics in Berlin in 2009.

event, and became the first Cypriot athlete to qualify for the final of the Gymnastics Grand Prix in Madrid. The Cyprus national shooting team also had a very successful year. Bianka Kassianidou won the gold medal in the skeet event at the world University games in Beijing as well as in the Commonwealth Games Shooting Championships that were held in Cyprus (team event). She also won a silver medal at the individual event. Eleni Artymata represented Cyprus at the 2008 Summer Olympics in Beijing. She competed at the 200 metres where she reached the second round. At the 2009 World Athletics Championships, in Berlin, she reached the final of the 200 metres where she finished eighth. In the field of tennis Cyprus has been represented in many international tournaments by Marcos Baghdatis who is a professional tennis player with many important victories and results in the past years. He is the only Cypriot ever to play in a Grand Slam tournament.

George Achilleos (centre) Gold Medal winner at the 2010 World Championships in Lonato, Italy.

World ranked tennis player Marcos Baghdatis playing in the Davis Cup tournament in Cyprus.

FOOTBALL

Football is the most popular sport in Cyprus. The Cyprus Football Association (CFA) was established in 1934 with the CFA organising various championships for its member clubs. In 1948, the Cyprus Football Association became a member of FIFA and in 1962 a member of UEFA. The Cyprus National Team played its first international game in 1949, at a time when Cyprus was not yet an independent state.

The CFA now participates at the national team level in the World Cup Competitions, the Olympic Tournaments and all the UEFA competitions for national teams (Senior, Under-21, Under-19, Under-17, Futsal and Women's). It also participates at the club level in the UEFA Club Competitions. In the 2008-2009 and 2009-2010 seasons two Cypriot clubs, "Anorthosis" of Famagusta and "Apoel" of Nicosia respectively, managed to qualify to the group stages of the UEFA Champions League. This was a major success for Cyprus.

There are currently fifty-seven clubs directly affiliated to the CFA and approximately two hundred and ninety indirectly affiliated clubs through local amateur associations. The CFA organises league championships of various levels and a cup competition. There are four divisions comprising of fourteen teams in each division. The CFA also organises women's and futsal championships.

The Cypriot Men's National Team before a World Cup qualifier against the Republic of Ireland at the GSP Stadium in Nicosia (5 September 2009).

NATIONAL PARALYMPIC COMMITTEE

The Cyprus National Paralympic Committee is the national constituent of the worldwide Paralympic movement and is subject to the controls of the International Paralympic Committee (IPC). It is responsible for organising the participation of Cypriot athletes in the Paralympic Games.

The Paralympic Games are a major international multi-sport event where athletes with physical disabilities including mobility disabilities, compete. There are Winter and Summer Paralympic Games, which are held immediately after the Olympic Games.

> Swimmer Karolina Pelendritou has represented Cyprus in many competitions and has won many medals.

Swimmer Karolina Pelendritou has represented Cyprus in many competitions and has won many medals. These include the gold medal in the 100m breaststroke at the 2004 Paralympic Games in Athens where Karolina won with a new Paralympic record.

Other achievements include a gold medal in the Eurowaves (European Cup) 2008 in the 100m breaststroke with a new world record and in the 2008 Beijing Paralympics. In the Beijing Paralympics Games she also won a bronze medal in the 200m individual medley.

More achievements have also been recorded by the athlete Antonis Aresti, who received several medals including silver medals in the 400m and 200m track races in the 2008 Beijing Paralympic Games.

Karolina Pelendritou at the 2008 Beijing Paralympic Games.

SPECIAL OLYMPICS

The Special Olympics Cyprus was inaugurated in 1986. It is a member of Special Olympics International and of the Cyprus Olympic Committee. It is recognised as the athletic organisation responsible for athletes with mental disabilities. It is a non-profit institution and its activities and games are organised by volunteers.

More than 400 athletes with mental and/or severe learning abilities train in sports such as swimming, cycling, basketball, football, gymnastics, riding, bowling, floor hockey, and sports for the handicapped. Athletes from Cyprus have won medals in European and world Sports events.

Special Olympics athletes.

culture

culture

CULTURE

Cultural life in Cyprus is promoted both by the government through the Cultural Services of the Ministry of Education and Culture and through private organisations and individuals.

The people of Cyprus are actively interested in encouraging creativity in the field of letters and arts, and in raising cultural awareness and making culture available to everyone, so that there is a greater participation of the public in the island's cultural life. The government also attaches great importance to the promotion of the culture of Cyprus abroad and in projecting cultural achievements in order to highlight Cyprus' links with international culture.

The art and culture of Cyprus goes beyond the ancient ruins, museums and numerous archeological sites.

Particular emphasis is placed on promoting literature, music, dance (modern and classical), the visual arts and cinema. In addition, a special arts festival (the «Kypria») is organised annually with a view to upgrading the artistic movement on the island. The festival, which is held in all major cities hosts artists and ensembles of international acclaim from Cyprus, Greece and other countries. Since its inception, in 1991, this has become a major institution making high quality cultural entertainment accessible to a wide range of people. The artistic performances include: theatre, ballet, opera and music. Alongside well-known international artists or ensembles, Cypriot artists who have distinguished themselves abroad and acquired international reputation are also invited to participate.

Stass Paraschos' outdoor art exhibition at Lemba, Pafos district.

Exhibits at the Limassol Sculpture Park.

Moreover, many permanent exhibitions are found in the many museums in Cyprus which exhibit ancient artefacts, paintings, sculpture, metal objects, ceramics, jewellery and objects of traditional art all of which witness different stages in the course of human presence on the island. The art and culture of Cyprus goes beyond the ancient ruins, museums and numerous archeological sites. Contemporary art is exhibited in the modern art museums in Nicosia and Limassol and a remarkable array of public sculptures commissioned by the Limassol Municipality can be found at the Limassol Sculpture Park featuring twenty large sculptures by artists from Greece, Israel, Germany, Egypt and Cyprus. Furthermore, the sculptural wall at Stass Paraskos' Cyprus College of Art in Lemba, in the Pafos district, created by the artist and his students, also makes up a permanent outdoor exhibition of artworks from recycled and discarded material and carved local stone.

The Miró Exhibition
in Nicosia (2010).

Additionally, Cyprus plays host to major international exhibitions. The Cultural Services organise exhibitions which come within the framework of exchange programmes with foreign countries or in collaboration with overseas museums and institutions of art. On 10 March 2010, "Miró of Majorca", possibly the most important art exhibition that ever came to Cyprus was inaugurated at the Nicosia Municipal Arts Centre (Old Power House) associated with the Pierides Foundation. This was the first time that an exhibition of such magnitude focusing on the work of a great single artist was organised on the island. The exhibition was realised in the framework of the Spanish Presidency of the European Union. The Spanish government dedicated the event to the Fiftieth Independence Anniversary of the Republic of Cyprus. Apart from the Nicosia Municipal Arts Centre and the Pierides Foundation, a series of significant institutions and organisations collaborated for the great success of this undertaking: the Ministry of Education and Culture (Cultural Services department), the Pilar I Joan Miró Foundation of Majorca, the Telloglio Foundation of the Aristotle University of Thessaloniki, the Spanish G government, the State Corporation for Spanish Cultural Action Abroad and the Cyprus Tourism Organisation.

> Queen Sofia of Spain accepted an invitation to visit Cyprus for the opening ceremony of the Miró Exhibition.

Queen Sofia of Spain accepted an invitation to visit Cyprus for the opening ceremony of this great cultural event. She is well known as a great patron of the arts and an art-lover herself. During her visit to Cyprus, she was accompanied by the Spanish Foreign Minister, Miguel Angel Moratinos, and was

An aspect of the Miró Exhibition, Nicosia (2010).

given a warm welcome at the Nicosia Municipal Arts Centre by the President of the Republic of Cyprus, Mr Demetris Christofias, many important personalities and a large crowd from all walks of life.

Queen Sofia of Spain with President Christofias and Mrs Elsi Christofias at the inauguration of the Miró Exhibition at the Nicosia Municipal Arts Centre (10 March 2010).

THE CULTURAL FOUNDATION

The eastern Mediterranean island of Cyprus has a cultural history that stretches back thousands of years. The ancient city kingdom of Salamis, for example, was home to one of the foremost cultural centres of its day. It had amongst others, an amphitheatre seating 20.000 spectators, and is just one of the ancient sites that offer evidence of the longstanding cultural importance of Cyprus and the region.

For a number of years, efforts have been ongoing to create a modern cultural centre in Cyprus that would recapture the glory days of the past and once again establish the island as a regional leader in cultural activities. To this end, the Cyprus Cultural Foundation was established in 2005 by the government and tasked with the creation of the Cyprus Cultural Centre in Nicosia, the island's capital.

Scheduled to open to the general public in 2014, the Cyprus Cultural Centre will be a national venue for the performing arts, in particular symphonic and chamber music, dance, opera and musical theatre. Located in the heart of Nicosia, close to the seat of government, the Presidential Palace, the new House of Representatives, the new State Theatre and the new State Art Gallery, the Cyprus Cultural Centre will be a perfect blend of form and function, combining architectural excellence and carefully considered functionality.

> Scheduled to open to the general public in 2014, the Cultural Centre will be a national venue for the performing arts, in particular symphonic and chamber music, dance, opera and musical theatre.

The Main Stage of the Cultural Centre to be completed in 2014.

Representing a significant cultural development for Cyprus, the Eastern Mediterranean and the wider European Union, the Centre will prove vital in meeting the expectations of increasingly discerning audiences as well as ensuring that Cyprus features prominently on the burgeoning landscape of cultural tourism. By showcasing the very best in local, regional and international talent, the Centre will become a cultural focal point for the region, offering local artists the opportunity to work alongside the best performers from all over the world.

As well as a concert hall, the Centre will also assume a vital role in the civic, social and educational fabric of Cyprus itself, serving as a focal point for

culture

The Concert Hall of the Cultural
Centre to be completed in 2014.

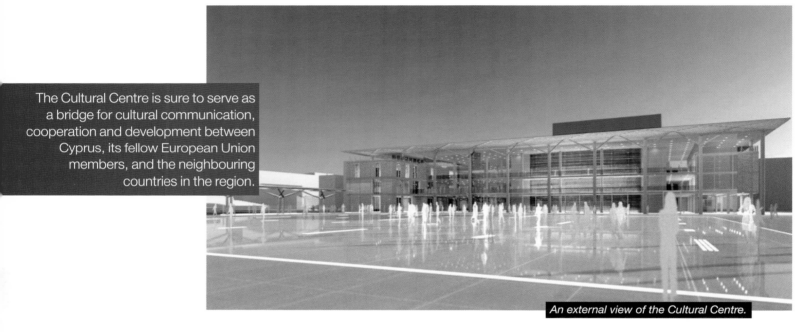

The Cultural Centre is sure to serve as a bridge for cultural communication, cooperation and development between Cyprus, its fellow European Union members, and the neighbouring countries in the region.

An external view of the Cultural Centre.

the performing arts while enhancing the overall development of cultural life on the island. In addition to attending performances, visitors will also be able to relax and socialise with friends and colleagues in the attractive gardens and central square.

Along with its main performance hall, the Centre will also boast a separate hall and an outdoor area, suitable for large scale concerts and other forms of popular entertainment. Other facilities will include areas dedicated to educational activities and social functions. By establishing the Centre as a multi-

purpose venue, the public will be encouraged to visit, and to attend performances and functions beyond those hosted in the main halls.

The establishment of the Cyprus Cultural Centre has already been hailed as the beginning of a cultural renaissance in Cyprus. The Centre is sure to serve as a bridge for cultural communication, cooperation and development between Cyprus, its fellow European Union members, and the neighbouring countries in the region.

The outdoor Sculpture Park in Limassol.

THE VISUAL ARTS (1960-2010)
AN OVERVIEW
Dr Eleni S.Nikita

Visual creation is today one of the most dynamic and vibrant fields of the artistic expression and life of Cyprus. Cypriots have demonstrated their morphoplastic abilities since antiquity, leaving us wonderful examples in all the fields of art.

Unfortunately, however, the island was not destined to enjoy long periods of peace, political stability and economic prosperity, essential prerequisites for the development, flowering and consolidation of indigenous artistic creation because her important geopolitical position made her the prey of those forces who wielded power in the region at different historical periods. Thus artistic expression was limited for a number of centuries to Byzantine – religious and folk art.

> The evolution of an art independent of folk and religious art was slow and was linked to the improvement in economic and social conditions on the island.

After Cyprus was ceded by the Ottomans to Great Britain, a limited interest began to be created in secular art, but this interest remained completely marginal for several decades. The evolution of an art independent of folk and religious art was slow and was linked to the improvement in economic and social conditions on the island, the gradual creation of a bourgeoisie and the rise in the educational standard of the people.

At the beginning of the twentieth century we have the first Cypriots who studied art abroad. However, up to the end of the Second World War, the artists who lived on the island were very few in number and movement in the visual arts was very limited.

The cultural and ideological climate of the period played a particularly important role in shaping the form and content of the art which developed during the first half of the twentieth century. Already, from the decade of the 1920s, the age-old desire of the Greek Cypriots for union with Greece had been rekindled.

An important aspect of the anti-colonial struggle against Britain and for union with Greece (1955 – 1959) was the assertion of "Greekness" as well as the reinforcement of the national identity. As a result, the first Greek Cypriot intellectual associations focused a large part of their efforts on research into history and folklore and the projection of the national and religious characteristics of the island. This ideological climate influenced both the literary and the artistic creation on the island. Artists such as Adamantios Diamantis, George Pol. Georghiou and Telemachos Kanthos, encouraged with their work the learning of the history, physiognomy and traditions of Cyprus, self-knowledge and the awareness of the identity of the Cypriots.

Of course, up to the end of the 1950s the number of artists living and working in Cyprus continued to be limited. The work of art had only very few consumers. In the decade of the 1950s Cypriot society was still mainly agrarian and functioned on the basis of the values of traditional closed societies. There was no historically established prosperous bourgeoisie which could have been the natural consumer and supporter of works of art and, moreover, the educational level of the people did not help their favourable reception.

These conditions, as well as the national liberation struggle of 1955-59, contributed to the complete isolation of the island and kept closed the lines of any artistic communication with the European centres of contemporary art and the new artistic currents which had begun to dominate the international artistic scene. The few artists who lived in Cyprus remained confined to the teachings of the Schools of Fine Art at which they had studied and especially to representational currents, and produced works which are characterised by trends which range from academicism to the movements of historical modernism.

The decade of the 1960s: the break of the old with the new and the prevalence of a new concept of art
This situation was to change radically after independence in 1960. According to the Constitution of the newly-founded state, education, culture and religion were not the concern of the central government but were to be directly handled by the Greek and Turkish Cypriot communities through their respective Communal Chambers.

After the intercommunal clashes which began in December 1963 and the withdrawal of the Turkish Cypriots from the government, Communal Chambers were dissolved. As a result the Ministry of Education was created in 1965 and the cultural development of Cyprus was entrusted to the Ministry's Cultural Services department. The interest of the State in letters and the arts gradually became institutionalised in order to serve a specific cultural policy. At the same time, the Republic of Cyprus began to create the necessary institutions which would allow it to function as an independent state.

The contribution of foreign embassies and particularly of the cultural sections or centres which some of them created, proved essential to the first opening up of Cyprus to contemporary western culture. The creation of the Ministry of Education and its department of Cultural Services gave new impetus to the visual arts scene in Cyprus, particularly as regards the projection of Cypriot art abroad, with the participation in various international exhibitions and biennials and the organisation abroad of exhibitions of the work of Cypriot artists. With the contribution of Tony Spiteris (then General Secretary of the International Union of Art Critics and advisor on art to the government), Cyprus became linked to major artistic events. Spiteris was conversant with the contemporary artistic trends and the spirit of quest which prevailed at international art exhibitions and, as was natural and to be expected, embraced a small group of young artists whose work represented the new trends on the island, reflected the same spirit and could be shown at these international openings, alongside the work of other contemporary artists. This attitude was also the cause for the first open clash between the new and the established in art.

> The need of the young artists to keep in step with the new currents in the visual arts was completely justified and expected.

The need of the young artists to keep in step with the new currents in the visual arts was completely justified and expected. Cyprus was now an independent state and its accession to Europe, where it naturally belonged, had to be actual and not just theoretical. This need was also gradually recognised by the State as one of the aims of state cultural policy, which changed towards the end of the 1960s in order to serve the broader pursuits and interests of an independent state.

The fact that the vast majority of those studying art in the 1950s and 1960s were at British Schools of Fine Art contributed to the creation of this new climate. On their return to Cyprus after completing their studies, these artists looked to the future with the almost sole intent of harmonising their artistic vocabularies with those prevailing on the international art scene. They questioned the conventional, introduced new modes of expression, new techniques and new materials. The new concepts which prevailed gave a new direction in the development of the arts.

An important personality of this period was Christophoros Savva (1924 – 1968) who was the connecting link between the art which developed in Cyprus before and after independence. Savva studied first in London and then in Paris. He had a powerful artistic presence and the frequent exhibitions of his work functioned as a catalyst for the creation of artistic movement in Cyprus. At the start of his career he created representational works based on the teachings of the fauvists, cubists and expressionists. He went on, however, to embrace the abstract movements, contributing substantially to the exploration of the values of non-representational art. He was also a pioneer in exploring the expressive potentials of materials, exploiting in his art materials like sacking, sand, dust, wood, some ready-made objects and others. As well as the means, he also broadened the forms of his expression and, alongside his painting, engaged in sculpture, relief, wall-painting, constructions and material collage. But whether he was using representational or a completely abstract

> It was at "Apophasis" that the first joint exhibition by Greek Cypriot and Turkish Cypriot artists was organised after the creation of the Republic of Cyprus.

language, a source of Savva's inspiration always remained the local material, the shapes, the colours and the light of his country.

In addition to his important work in art, Savva was also a cultural catalyst, gathering round him young people of the arts and letters, first by establishing in 1955 the Pancyprian Union of Art Lovers and later, in 1960, the "Apophasis" gallery, which operated as a professional gallery and also as a cultural centre, organising a large number of cultural events.

It was at "Apophasis" that the first joint exhibition by Greek Cypriot and Turkish Cypriot artists was organised after the creation of the Republic of Cyprus. The Turkish Cypriot artists Djevded Chagdash, Fikri Tirekoglou, Ismet Guney and Soferoglou took part in the exhibition. This exhibition received very favourable comments. The magazine "Nea Epochi" had this to say: *"It is the first time that a meeting takes place at a joint event outside the conventional cooperation which flows from the state regime into other fields. The artists by themselves, freely, found the common points of contact, and art is the best means of contact, of all people of any race, ideology or religion. This new event which was presented at the initiative of the gallery is important."*

It should be noted here that the visual arts in the Turkish Cypriot community had followed a completely different course than in the Greek Cypriot community. The Islamic tradition, which forbade the depiction of figures, and the close relationship of the Turkish Cypriot community with Turkey, which was linked

Christoforos Savva, "The Poet's Tomb",
oil and sand on sack, 60x79cm, (1962).
Collection of Renos Siman.

to European art after 1923, essentially slowed the development of contemporary visual arts in the Turkish Cypriot community. As a result, the Turkish Cypriot community produced very few artists in the 1960s. Apart from the four referred to previously, mention must be made of Ayhan Mentesh, who in 1962 exhibited at the Commonwealth Institute in London together with Adamantios Diamantis, George Pol. Georghiou and Christophoros Savva. Also, in the State Collection of works of contemporary Cypriot art there are works by Yilmaz Hakeri and Hasan Amir which were purchased before 1974.

As we proceed to the end of the 1960s, the dominance of the new spirit in art is continuously strengthened. Among the first to embrace the abstract currents were Andreas Chrysochos (1929), and Stelios Votsis (1929), who were interested in a new art, a vehicle of intellectual quests and values, ridding their painting of every kind of "atmosphere" and subjective references. Mikis Michaelides (1923) moved over to abstraction very early on and from the beginning of the 1960s concentrated on the creation of relief sculptures and three dimensional works on stretched canvas. In the same period, Marios Loizides (1928-1989) would produce with a strict abstract geometric vocabulary, work which was the result of vision, while Vera Gavrielidou-Hadjida (1936) produced work in which the abstraction is based on allusion and instinct, later going on to embrace movements such as post-painterly abstraction and op art. Katy Stephanidou (1925), with constructivist forms as a starting point,

would proceed to completely abstract painting, while Costas Ioachim focused his exploration on the development of fluid linear subjects. In 1972 he placed his painting in space, creating one of the first environmental works. An important role in the dominance of abstract discourse was played by two British artists who settled in Cyprus: Glyn Hughes (1931) and John Corbidge (1935-2003).

Apart from the artists who studied in Britain, other artists who had studied in other European countries also turned to the abstract currents, for example Anna Constantinou (1947) who studied in Rome, Stella Michaelidou (1941) who studied in Athens and Paris, Mikis Phinikarides (1940-2005) who studied in Athens and Constantinos Yannikouris (1939) who studied in Paris.

As we approach the close of the 1960s, we see abstract visual discourse dominating. The artists adopted the geometrical vocabularies, minimal art, post-painterly abstraction, op art, constructivism, art informel, the hard edge and generally attached more importance to their artistic vocabulary and less to the subject. Also, their language of expression was enriched with new quests. Andreas Ladommatos (1940) produced at the end of the 1960s a series of constructivist reliefs and constructions to which he would later introduce movement, producing some of the first kinetic works (with an electric motor) and works with moving lights in Cypriot art.

Angelos Makrides (1942) and George Sfikas (1943) would take important steps in reducing to the minimum their means of expression and from the end

> An important role in the dominance of abstract discourse was played by two British artists who settled in Cyprus: Glyn Hughes (1931) and John Corbidge (1935-2003).

Stelios Votsis, "Geometric", silkscreen print, 129x69cm, (1969). Collection of Yiorgos and Tonia Loizou.

of the decade of the 1960s would turn their attention to projecting the concepts which reside in the work of art, arriving even at statements where the concept is reduced to a work of art. Nikos Kouroushis (1937) was also occupied with constructions and with the exploration of the real space. In 1970 he presented his work "Action", which was completed by a performance in which the public participated. At the beginning of the decade of the 1970s there were also the first happenings from Antonis Antonios and Glyn Hughes.

Beyond the abstract, geometrical and minimalist vocabularies, Cypriot artists also explored other forms of expression such as surrealism. Yiorgos Skotinos (1937) recast in a surrealist style images of the subconscious which are raked up together with primitive cultural symbols and primeval myths of the ancestral land. Rhea Bailey (1946) and Maria Tourou (1943) also expressed themselves with surrealistic vocabulary.

In order to concentrate on the essential and archetypal, Stass Paraschos (1933) consciously adopted an unsophisticated and naive artistic vocabulary with expressionist and fauvist forms and depicted in representational language subjects from history and the life of his country. At the same time, a group of artists continued along the paths which the fathers of Cypriot art had forged and with renewed representational forms painted the people and the landscape of Cyprus. Among these artists are Lefteris Economou (1930-2007), Costas Economou (1925), Eleni Harikleidou (1926-1978) and Dora Farmaka (1937).

Emin Cizenel, "Spring", mixed
media on canvas, (2003).

Asik Mene, "Checkpoint", oil on
canvas, 150x200cm, (2004).

Nikos Kouroushis,
Performance, audience
participation.

Stass Paraschos, "Liberty Abandons Cyprus", oil on canvas,140x153cm, (1972). Collection of Pefkios and Margarita Georgiades.

The same course to abstraction was followed by Cypriot sculpture which was influenced for the most part by the trends and currents prevailing in Britain, the country where most of the sculptors studied. They were influenced in particular by the sculpture of the vital, organic, biomorphic form whose main exponent was Henry Moore, by the sculpture of constructivism and by the simplified geometric shapes with coloured surfaces of the artists of the "New Generation".

Andreas Savvides (1930), the first sculptor to study in London, would be influenced first by Henry Moore and Barbara Hepworth and, later, from 1969, would produce a series of constructivist, minimalist works, based on the relationships of geometric shapes. With these brightly coloured sculptures he comes very close to the artists of the "New Generation" group. It is the same with George Sfikas (1943) who explores the relations of the space with absolute geometric shapes and colour. Later, Sfikas would concentrate on and express in Cyprus the values of conceptual art. Yiorgos Kyriakou (1940) would be interested first in biomorphic sculpture and then would draw his shapes from the traditional tools and the folk art in general of his native land.

Demetris Constantinou (1924) would also move within the geometric vocabulary and the spirit of constructivism. He studied in Alexandria. In contrast, Andis Hadjiadamos (1936-1990) had as his starting point the organic world, biomorphic shapes and

> Among the sculptors mention should also be made of Valentinos Charalambous (1929), who engaged particularly in monumental ceramics, characterised by the values of abstraction and by high technique.

African art. Nikos Dymiotis (1930-1990), Andreas Farmakas (1938) and Aristides Anastasiades (1940) would experiment with many types of sculpture, both realistic and abstract.

Among the sculptors mention should also be made of Valentinos Charalambous (1929), who engaged particularly in monumental ceramics, characterised by the values of abstraction and by high technique.

The new trends which gradually began to appear at the beginning of the decade of the 1960s crystallised completely at the start of the 70s. The new artists were increasingly active and artistic movement intensified.

The 1970s: the course is overturned
This course was violently halted in July 1974 by the coup d'état against the elected president of Cyprus and by Turkey's military invasion of the island that followed. The new reality fundamentally changed the priorities of the government and the people.

Artistic and cultural life in general came to a standstill. Artists and creators in general were at a loss in the face of these events. The experiential relationship with the historic event would unavoidably overturn the course of Cypriot contemporary art. The world of art would be linked indirectly or directly, consciously or unconsciously, with it. The insistence on form in the shapes and on colour which characterised the new trends would be set aside, with interest returning to the subject and the message. The artist desired to communicate through the most easily comprehensible messages, to narrate, record, accuse. Many resorted

to realistic forms of expression and others inserted representational themes among abstract motifs, often with symbolic connotations.

In the decade of the 1970s another change crystallised which concerned the country of study of artists. Britain no longer monopolised the student of art, who turned to countries with which the Republic of Cyprus had developed friendly relations such as France, Italy, the Soviet Union and the communist countries of Eastern Europe. This trend would be strengthened after 1974, as a result of the scholarships and facilities which these countries gave to the Cypriot people who were suffering in the aftermath of the Turkish invasion and occupation. Greece, of course, continued to remain a very popular destination for study.

It must be mentioned that the Cypriot artists are compelled to study in schools abroad since Cyprus does not have a School of Fine Art. This was definitive in the shaping of the aesthetic identity of contemporary Cypriot art because it hindered the creation of a national school of art. At the same time, however, it helped significantly the opening of a continuous and fertile dialogue with European art. Cypriot artists studied in various aesthetic and ideological environments and on their return to Cyprus created their own artistic vocabulary, embarking on their course from different starting points.

The decade of the 1980s: plurality of stylistic and morphoplastic directions

A result of the increase in centres of study, the increased possibilities of artists participating in international art exhibitions and the easier access to information and knowledge, was the plurality of styles and morphoplastic directions, which is one of the main characteristics of the art which developed during the 1980s. On their return to Cyprus, after completing their studies, the artists bonded with their historical-social reality, local artistic memories and tradition, the particularity of the light, the colour of the masses and shapes of the natural environment of Cyprus and later, after a creative osmosis with their acquired artistic knowledge, proceeded in search of their own artistic vocabulary.

The conversation between these exogenous and endogenous factors which is conducted at a personal level for each artist, determined the polymorphism which characterises contemporary Cypriot art. If we look at the works produced by the generation which completed their studies at the end of the 1960s and in the 1970s and 1980s, it is not difficult to discern the great broadening of morphoplastic developments of theoretical and aesthetic references and of the stimulating subject matter which substantially enriched Cypriot art.

In the history of contemporary Cypriot art, the decade of the 1980s must also be recorded as the one during which a real renewal of the artistic vocabulary is observed, as well as of the thematic and semantic content of the work of art. The artistic scene was enriched with new blood and a new dynamism in art was created. From the beginning of the 1980s,

> Cypriot artists are compelled to study in schools abroad since Cyprus does not have a School of Fine Art. This was definitive in the shaping of the aesthetic identity of contemporary Cypriot art because it hindered the creation of a national school of art.

the majority of the artists returning to Cyprus were born in the 1950s and they reinstated in their own way the earlier demand of the artists of the 60s for renewal of the form of art and the redefinition of its values (Theodoulos Gregoriou, Maria Loizidou, Koula Savvidou, Ioannis, Glafkos Koumides, Hélène Black, Eleni Nicodemou, Savvas Christodoulides, Stavros Antonopoulos and others).

Some of these artists gave importance to symbolism, to the inner energy and the expressiveness of materials, to the exploration of cultural values, philosophical thought and to the primitive myths. They exploited modern technologies, expressed themselves for the most part with constructions and installations in space and created works which re-shape contemporary reality and involve the viewer in a dialogue, provoking his critical thought.

> Some artists gave importance to symbolism, to the inner energy and the expressiveness of materials, to the exploration of cultural values, philosophical thought and to the primitive myths.

From the middle of the 1980s Cyprus resumed its links with important international art events and participated in new ones, a fact which signalled the start of the presence of Cypriot artists on the international art scene, a presence which would go on to become more marked.

Redefinition of the values of art
The great national disaster of 1974 and the continuing political crisis affected and is still affecting significantly the trends, character, orientations and generally the values of contemporary Cypriot art. The external threats and the danger of national extinction

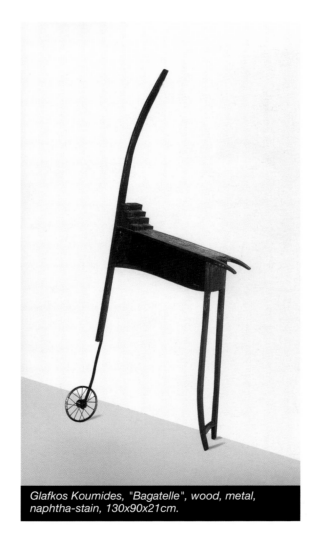

Glafkos Koumides, "Bagatelle", wood, metal, naphtha-stain, 130x90x21cm.

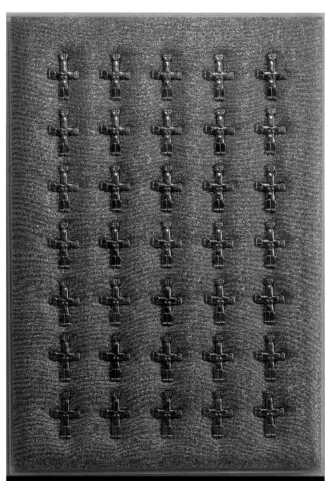

Hélène Black, "Strange Bedfellows", cast aluminium, foam insulating material, plexiglass,150x100x8cm, (2006). CYTA collection.

led to the re-examination and redefinition of many social and individual ideologies and attitudes and also re-determined the stance of many artists vis à vis their personal creation. The continuation of the Cyprus political crisis, which intensified the need for preserving national characteristics, the crisis of values which art internationally was going through with the re-instatement of many principles and the reassessment of national particularities which took place in a new spirit without ethnocentricity and rejection of the foreign, forced a number of Cypriot artists to fall back on the sources of their own space, creatively activating local material. Thus, simultaneously with the subject matter, an aesthetic began to take shape which, in parallel with the acquisitions of western art, fertilised morphoplastically, and in particular, conceptually and symbolically, elements of the indigenous artistic memory. In its best realisations, this trend succeeded in producing works which, although characterised by a spirit of the place, have universal dimensions.

> The external threats and the danger of national extinction led to the re-examination and redefinition of many social and individual ideologies and attitudes and also re-determined the stance of many artists vis à vis their personal creation.

The turn, however, towards local material, now happened at a completely different level. There was no longer an equation of personal with group mythology, of individual with collective conscience, as there was in the past. The works no longer constitute the synopsis of the indigenous characteristics of the Cypriot space and so they have lost their monumental and their epic nature. All the process is now carried out at the conscious level of the creator, who expresses personal and no longer group mythologies. The shift in weight from the collective and external to the individual and internal is a more general principle which also characterises other major achievements of the Cypriot art of today. The piecemeal stirring up, through the indigenous iconoplastic memory, of images which function in order to express emotions of the present, the exploitation of archetypes, the use of old materials or objects with inner, eternal energy, the approach to the subject through symbols, concepts, philosophical and scientific theories and their remoulding and expression consciously or automatically through the existential conscience of the creator, is one of the most interesting directions of the Cypriot visual art of the 1980s and 1990s.

> The shift in weight from the collective and external to the individual and internal is a more general principle which also characterises other major achievements of the Cypriot art of today.

Continuing this brief historical reading of the Cypriot contemporary art created in the 1980s and 1990s, we see yet another general trend crystallising with increasing clarity. The relationship between artistic creation and the destiny of the island, which intervenes actively, influences the young artist more or less obviously. The trials and tribulations the country was going through, the daily feeling of insecurity and suspense, the waiting and the uncertain tomorrow which were experienced at a conscious or unconscious level and which were reinforced by other pessimistic universal messages, created a spiritual anguish which was reflected in artistic creation as existential agony, as a dialogue between life and death. This trend linked Cypriot art with some prevailing forms of contemporary international art, which do not want

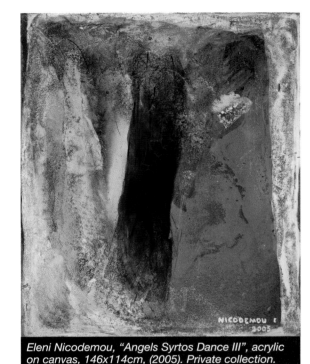

Eleni Nicodemou, "Angels Syrtos Dance III", acrylic on canvas, 146x114cm, (2005). Private collection.

artistic creation to be isolated but, involving it in a wider spectrum, transform it into reader, theoretician, exponent, "poet" and exorciser of the present and omen of the future.

The artistic vocabulary is being renewed and broadened continuously. From the middle of the 1980s a number of artists showed a particular preference for the exploration of the potential of materials and

for the energy which the work of art creates. Thus, we had an increasing number of constructions and installations in space. Apart from Nicos Kouroushis, Angelos Markides and George Sfikas, who belonged to an older generation, several new artists renounced the illusion of the painting space in order to set their work in the real space, thus multiplying the stimuli of the viewer.

There were, however, a number of artists who continued to remain faithful to the values of painting and of the two-dimensional picture. With various gestures and vocabularies which reveal their constant contact with the world-wide artistic scene, they produced their own mythologies. Many younger artists, born after 1970, also remained faithful to painting. They painted in a spirit of quest, trying to renew their morphoplastic language continuously. Also, a number of artists of the new generation used mixed media and experimented, in addition to painting, with photography, constructions, installations in space, video and new technology.

All these artists who set out in the 1980s are the main shapers of the Cypriot artistic scene of today.

The twenty-first century and the accession of Cyprus to the European Union

The twenty-first century opens up new prospects for contemporary Cypriot art. On 1 May 2004 Cyprus became a full member of the European Union. The Cypriot artist feels less and less isolated. The opportunities for collaboration with other European artists are multiplying. The Cypriot artist takes part in European art programmes and benefits substantially from the European Union policy on the mobility of artists and works of art within the European geographical space. Many artists are invited by major museums, international art organisations and well-known curators of exhibitions to show their work. Some of them are creating a career outside Cyprus as well.

The Cypriot artist is beginning, day by day, to feel a resident of Europe and to wish to share with other Europeans common problems and visions. He wants to meet them, tries to empathise with their own socio-political problems, to recognise, over and above his cultural particularities, the values and the cultural elements he shares with them. He ascertains that many of the issues which occupy him are identical to those of his European colleagues and is becoming aware that Cyprus is a microcosm of many phenomena which are observed today on a European and world-wide scale.

> The Cypriot artist takes part in European art programmes and benefits substantially from the European Union policy on the mobility of artists and works of art within the European geographical space.

Apart from the accession of Cyprus to the European Union, the twenty-first century is also characterised by another important event which affects artistic creation. In May 2003, the first of the road blocks dividing Cyprus since 1974 and Nicosia since 1963 opened. Communication – under certain conditions of course – between free Cyprus and the occupied areas is now possible. The young Cypriot artist is discovering the other "unknown" half of his country which for years was cut off, the lost part, the wound in the body of individual and national self-knowledge. He is also discovering, however, a truth to which he has to become reconciled. This "other half", this piece of the country, of his national history and his personal roots, will perhaps remain a loss, an absence, forever. He has to respect the new political situation, to accept the altered face of the "other half", to respect the new religious and social realities which colonisation by Turkey has created and at the same time to see the Turkish Cypriots as brothers. As inhabitants of the same motherland.

> The young Cypriot artist is discovering the other "unknown" half of his country which for years was cut off, the lost part, the wound in the body of individual and national self-knowledge. He is also discovering, however, a truth to which he has to become reconciled.

The subject matter of the artists has been affected decisively. However, although their work is frequently inspired by the politico-social and cultural particularities of their country, it expresses universal anxieties, problems, visions, concepts and values which also occupy their European colleagues. In the thematology of the Cypriot artist are detected the situations he is experiencing and the feelings which inhabit him. The loss, violent deprivation, dismemberment, being a refugee, insecurity, traumatic memory, fragmentation, removal, the concept of borders, nostalgia, absence, uprooting. These subjects he shares of course with other European artists who have lived through similar experiences.

Apart from these themes which are linked to the politico-social particularities of his country and define his particular mentality, the Cypriot artist is also sensitive to other subjects which characterise contemporary societies and today occupy artists all

Christos Foukaras, "St George", oil, 120x76cm, (1987).

over the planet. Subjects which flow from the quest for identity, the need for communication, alienation, difference, fluidity, the natural and intellectual environment, migration, globalisation, the lack of ecological conscience, extreme consumerism, the release from social and personal stereotypes, the role in and the relationship of art with society and politics occupy him in the same way as they do his European colleagues. Thus the local and the universal engage and define his work.

As regards the artistic vocabulary, there is no longer the distance and delay in time in the adoption of avant garde forms of expression as there was in the past. The Cypriot creator uses the same contemporary means and exploits technology as competently. The young artists express themselves more and more with installations in space, happenings, performances, video or video installations, digital art and generally exploit all the means which new technologies offer them. Many show a preference for the work in progress, the open work with rich or, better, with open semiotics. Thus, the viewer is involved more and more in the completion of the work.

The abolition of some of the restrictions in the movement between the free and the occupied areas of the Republic of Cyprus is bringing Greek Cypriot and Turkish Cypriot artists together. They are discovering each other's art and are beginning to organise joint exhibitions. The Cyprus government supports financially and morally these joint endeavours. It is indicative that in 2007 Cyprus was represented at the Venice Biennale by the work of a Greek Cypriot and a Turkish Cypriot artist.

A general finding in this brief, synoptic and unavoidably fragmentary reading of the art which has developed in Cyprus after 1960 till today is that the particular conditions of the island (historical, social, economic, cultural and geographical) played a definitive role in its character and particular identity. Indisputably, the Cypriot artist of today reveals to us his cultural and personal conscience and his experiential relationship with social and political events which he reshapes, recreates in open works of art, to involve the viewer as much as possible.

A second general finding is the breadth of the aesthetic and theoretical references which distinguish the work of the Cypriot artist with which he still shows today the ability which he has had since antiquity for communication, dialogue with different cultural systems and also the ability to compose and create works with their own particularity and identity.

In conclusion, the special mark of Cypriot art today is its vitality and its power of renewal, characteristics which perhaps in the future will contribute to the redefining of the established relationship of the centre with the fringe.

> The abolition of some of the restrictions in the movement between the free and the occupied areas of the Republic of Cyprus is bringing Greek Cypriot and Turkish Cypriot artists together.

*Andreas Savva, "Martyrologio",
installation, (2009).*

Nikos Charalambides, "The Sharing Project", installation, (2004).

*Angelos Makrides,
"The Great Greek
Encyclopedia", mixed
media, variable
dimensions, (1972).*

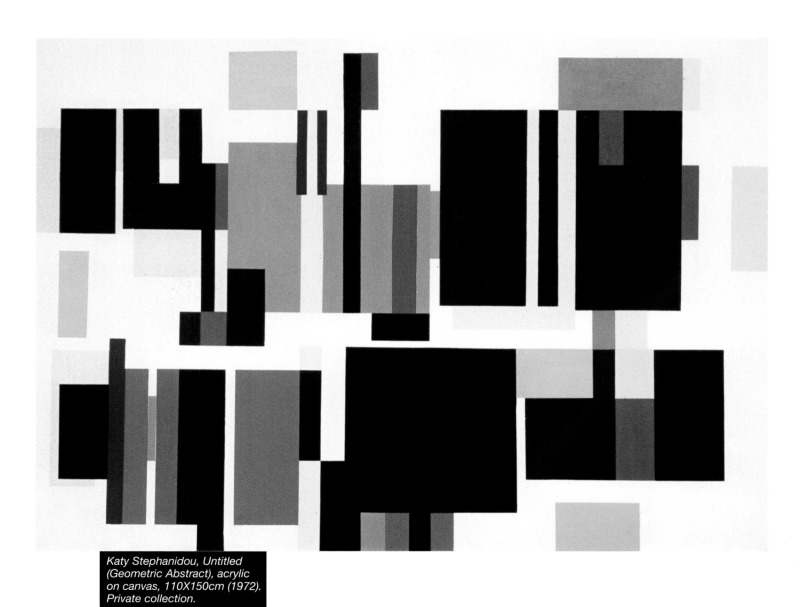

Katy Stephanidou, Untitled
(Geometric Abstract), acrylic
on canvas, 110X150cm (1972).
Private collection.

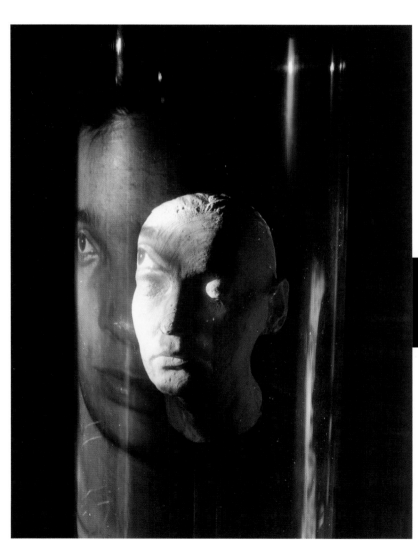

Yioula Hadjigeoghiou, "Labyrinth", (from the series "Where is my Head?"), installation, plexiglass pillar, head cast, projection, motion apparatus, 200x30cm, (2003). State Collection of Contemporary Cypriot Art.

Lia Lapithi, "Recipe for Marinated Crushed Olives", video, 3 minutes, (2006). Centre Pompidou collection, France.

Theodoulos Gregoriou, "Système Global XII", installation, Contemporary Art Centre, Nicosia. 5 spheres, 3 TV monitors glass, metal colour earth, slide projection.

culture
cyprus in the
venice
biennale of visual arts
1968-2010

CYPRUS IN THE VENICE
BIENNALE OF VISUAL ARTS (1968-2010)
Louli Michaelidou

The Venice Biennale of Contemporary Art was founded in 1895. It is the world's oldest international biennial and the only artistic event of this scale to maintain the system of national representations to this day.

As a young Republic, Cyprus participated in the Venice biennial for the first time in 1968, with six young artists: Christoforos Savva, Yiorgos Skotinos, George Kyriakou, Stelios Votsis, Costas Joachim and Andreas Chrysochos, presented some of the most pioneering work on the Cypriot scene at the time, reflecting its gradual infusion with various modernist movements. In the absence of a public institution for cultural affairs, this first exhibition was assigned to Tony Spiteris, a Greek art critic based in Venice, then acting as advisor to the Cyprus Republic, who set up the show inside a small storage space in the back of the Italian Pavilion.

> 1972 marked the last appearance of Cypriot artists in Venice before a long pause, due to the military invasion of Cyprus by Turkey in 1974.

1972 marked the last appearance of Cypriot artists in Venice before a long pause, due to the military invasion of Cyprus by Turkey in 1974. Although there was no official Cypriot participation that year, Costas Averkiou, Stelios Votsis, Nikos Kouroushis, Angelos Makrides and others contributed works to a specialised section of the biennial devoted to Engraving.

Poster – Cyprus Pavilion, Venice Biennale (2007).

The comeback was made in 1986 with Maria Loizidou, and, with one exception in 1995, Cyprus has since enjoyed an uninterrupted representation by some of its most prominent artists, like Angelos Makrides (1988), Theodoulos Gregoriou (1990, in *Aperto* – by invitation of the Biennial), Nikos Kouroushis (1990), Giorgos Sfikas (1993), Nikos Charalambidis,

cyprus in the
venice
biennale of visual arts
1968-2010

Cyprus in Venice

gravy planet

A World Drawing by
Panayiotis Michael and Konstantia Sofokleous

12 June - 6 November 2005
Opening hours: Tuesday - Sunday 10:00 - 18:00 / Monday closed
www.cyprusinvenice.com

REPUBLIC OF CYPRUS
Ministry of Education and Culture

A view of the Cyprus Pavilion, Venice Biennale (2005).

261

culture
cyprus in the
venice
biennale of visual arts
1968-2010

Lefteris Olympios, Theodoulos Gregoriou and Savvas Christodoulidis (1997), Glafkos Koumides (1999) and Andreas Karayan (2001). Up to this point, the artists were selected by an experts committee assigned by the Ministry. By the following edition, the notion of an open artistic competition was introduced, through which a curator of an international outlook and activity would be invited to select the participating artist(s). This change of policy aimed to enhance transparency, as well as upgrade the profile of the national pavilion and better promote the work of the artists abroad.

Cyprus was not among the countries to secure a permanent pavilion from the outset. The first Cypriot shows were accommodated either in the Giardini or the Arsenale, the two official biennial sites, depending on availability. From 1997 until 2003 (when Nikos Charalambidis returned for a solo show), Cyprus was exhibiting in various historic buildings around town, until the national pavilion found a more permanent roof in Palazzo Malipiero, centrally located by the Grand Canal near l' *Accademia*. The venue has successfully hosted the Cypriot presentations in 2005 (Panayiotis Michael and Konstantia Sofokleous), 2007 (Haris Epaminonda and Mustafa Hulusi) and 2009 (Socratis Socratous), and is already secured for the next three editions of the event.

> The Venice Biennale currently attracts nearly half a million visitors, and continues to constitute the biggest and most important international event of contemporary art in which the Republic of Cyprus participates.

Today, thirty-four countries exhibit in national pavilions in the Giardini, and over fifty others around the city. The Venice Biennale currently attracts nearly half a million visitors, and continues to constitute the biggest and most important international event of contemporary art in which the Republic of Cyprus participates.

Poster – Cyprus Pavilion, Venice Biennale (2003).

cyprus in the
venice
biennale of visual arts
1968-2010

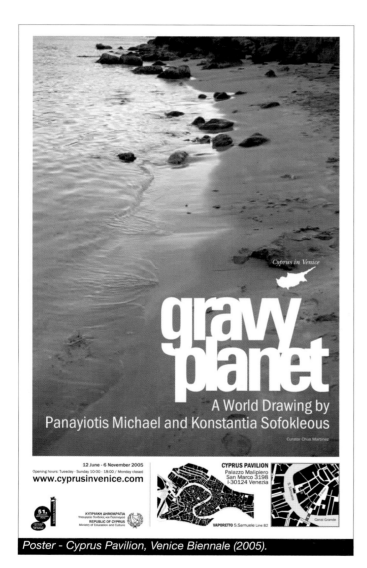

Poster - Cyprus Pavilion, Venice Biennale (2005).

Poster - Cyprus Pavilion, Venice Biennale (2009).

263

Thodosis Pierides

LITERATURE: AN OVERVIEW (1960-2010)
GREEK CYPRIOT LITERATURE
Lefkios Zafiriou

The official proclamation of the Republic of Cyprus on 16 August 1960 marks a new period for literature. The historical conditions, the almost belligerent atmosphere from 1963 till the invasion by Turkey in 1974, with its tragic consequences, had a direct influence on literary creation. The magazines *Pnevmatiki Kypros, Kypriaka Chronika, Nea Epochi* and *Epitheorisis Logou kai Technis* were the literary publications at the start of the new state. In *Kypriaka Chronika* in particular, young authors collaborated to produce work orientated to modernistic quests. Limited space does not permit the analytical presentation of more authors and their work and, instead of an extensive list of names, it was thought preferable to concentrate in this article on writers who in the main appear after 1960 and who together make up the "canon" of contemporary Cypriot literature.

> In the late period of British rule, Nicos Nicolaides (1884-1956) stands out with his prose, avant-garde for the era in which it was written, and so does Loukis Akritas (1909-1964) with his remarkable narrative work.

Giorgos Philippou Pierides

In the late period of British rule, Nicos Nicolaides (1884-1956) stands out with his prose, avant-garde for the era in which it was written, and so does Loukis Akritas (1909-1964) with his remarkable narrative work. Glafkos Alithersis (1897-1965) is the first poet to produce work worthy of note in the Pan-Hellenic community, while Tefkros Anthias (1903-1968) and Thodosis Pierides (1908-1968) continue from the inter-war period to write their socially committed poetry. In Th. Pierides' *Daydreaming on the Walls*

Costas Montis

of Famagusta (1965), the poetic narrative focuses on the history of the island as well as on the poetic struggles and quests of the creator himself. Nicos Vrahimis (1914-1961), with his innovative prose and Manos Kralis (1914-1989) with his poetry orientate Cypriot literature towards new horizons. Two writers, Giorgos Philippou Pierides (1904-1999) and Costas Montis (1914-2004), appear at this time and will go on to achieve remarkable work.

C. Montis, with three collections of poetry *(Moments* 1958, *Supplement to Moments* 1960 and *Poetry of Costas Montis* 1962) finalises the modernistic orientation in his poetry. The moments, poems of a few lines of transformed philosophical thought, constitute, as Alexis Zeras writes, a quite subversive contribution to the shaping of the poetics of the fragment. The collections of poems *Letter to Mother and Other Verses* (1965) and *Second Letter to Mother* (1972) are consummate achievements. In *Second*

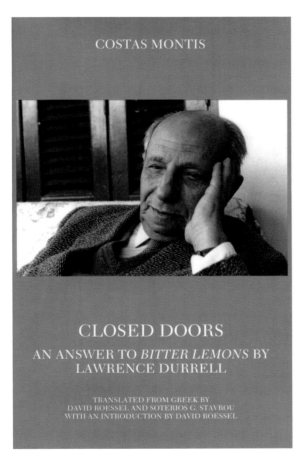

COSTAS MONTIS

CLOSED DOORS

AN ANSWER TO *BITTER LEMONS* BY
LAWRENCE DURRELL

TRANSLATED FROM GREEK BY
DAVID ROESSEL AND SOTERIOS G. STAVROU
WITH AN INTRODUCTION BY DAVID ROESSEL

with originality he records aspects of contemporary life and history with humour, irony and hyperbole. The collective national experience and his personal experience co-exist in his poetry with expressive accuracy and originality. In his work he gives voice in a unique manner to contemporary Cypriot anguish within the bounds of a human dimension and ethos. It is not fortuitous in any case that the sorrow of Cyprus also exists very clearly in his prose works. With his novella *Closed Doors* (1964) – a reply to Durrell's Bitter Lemons – his idiosyncratic modernistic narrative discourse acquires recognition through the distilled personal knowledge of the experience of the anti-colonial liberation struggle of 1955-1959 with linguistic and narrative vividness. In his novel *Mr Battistas and the Others* he succeeds in linking the present and the past through autobiographical and historical flashbacks in which legends and popular tales are intertwined. The poems in the Cypriot vernacular give a special note to his work.

Pantelis Mechanikos (1926-1979) was a poet of only a few poems. From the time when he started writing in 1957 until *Deposition* (1975), he moves in the climate of controversy. The poet-narrator, with satire and sarcasm, expresses anguish and stress, while in the quest for existential redemption the consciousness of the tragic aspect of history in his native land leads him to a more direct use of the language – raw quite often. Already from 1957, the title of his first collection *Deviations* hints at the diversification of Mechanikos as regards quests for themes and modes of expression, while with *The Two Mountains*, where the tragic sense of recent history is apparent, the poetic discourse acquires clearer expression. In *Deposition*

Pantelis Mechanikos

Letter to Mother in particular, the poetic discourse is expressed as a distillation of pain experienced at a personal and collective level and describes the depth of the human ordeal with accuracy and originality. His later collections garner a mature poetic harvest, where

265

(where the persona of Rimacho is used in a new poetic interpretation) he proceeded to an assessment of the Cyprus tragedy in strongly critical discourse and with anger and irony as the chief characteristics. Apart from the first poem in the collection, *"Ode to a Dead Young Turk"* written in April 1964, the rest constitute a poetic unity where the anguished tone of a bitter lyricism comes out indisputably as also the ultimate political protest.

Theodosis Nicolaou

Theodosis Nicolaou (1930-2004), in a distilled poetic discourse blends the bitter historical facts and the metaphysical quest in perfect lyrical poems. In his collections *Acta* (1980), Images (1988) and *The House* (1993, 2002), the poetic maturity through discourse which is plain and familiar leads to a contemplative viewing of things with linguistic immediacy and undecorated style its main traits. Moreover, his personal experiences, in combination with the collective ones of his native land, end up in poems in which the essential and the crucial comes first. The existential anguish, memory, love and Cyprus are the basic elements of the poetic mythology of Nicolaou. His last poetic composition stands out for its pointed and accurate language. In general, his poetry, abstract, contemplative and unadorned, marks with its modernistic orientation an earthly discourse despite its metaphysical wrappings.

Andreas Pastellas (1932) voices in his first collection of poems *Space of Diaspora* (1970) the frustrations of his generation in the first years of independence, after the 1955-59 freedom struggle. The allegory, satire and irony reveal, behind a feigned complacency, the alienation. In the collection *Posthumously Defrocked*

(1975) the accurate critical glance, in sarcastic vein, pre-supposes a human attitude which arises as the counterpoint to the disorientation of society.

Phivos Stavrides (1938) in the collection *Demystification* (1978) criticises in an angry voice the apathy in the face of the tragic reality after the Turkish invasion. With its immediacy and succinctness, with influences from M. Anagnostakis, his poetry is expressed as social and political protest. In the collection *Third Person* (1992), deviating from his earlier poetry, he crystallises a mature writing, assimilating fertile influences from C.P.Cavafy and other poets.

Kyriakos Charalambides (1940) already produces seminal poetry in his first collections. In the collection *The Vase with Designs* (1973) the epigrammatic discourse, with the inventiveness/ originality and the humour, characterises the singular lyric voice of the poet, who

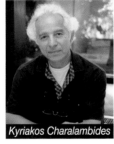

Kyriakos Charalambides

contemplates in depth his contemporary historical reality and anxiety. The persona of Rimacho acquires special interest in his poetry and for modern Cypriot poetry as well. The poems of the collection *Achaean Shore* (1977) mainly have the tragic events of 1974 as the central theme. The lyricism and the irony with dense discourse weave the heart-rending confession of the poet. The bitter taste of the war and its consequences are also present in the collection *Famagusta Regal Capital* (1982). The lyrical narrative,

KYRIAKOS CHARALAMBIDES

MYTHS AND HISTORY

SELECTED POEMS

SELECTED AND TRANSLATED FROM THE GREEK BY
DAVID CONNOLLY

WITH AN INTRODUCTION BY
THEOFANIS G. STAVROU

depicts contemporary reality with a plethora of symbols and rhythms. Apart from the drama of the missing (*Dome*, 1989), in his subsequent collections as well Charalambides describes the drama of Cyprus with references to myth and to history (*Dokimin*, 2000), giving ecumenical extensions to his poetry, while in *Quince Apple* (2006) Cavafian irony and the settled mature voice are the primary characteristics of a poetry with rare originality and linguistic profundity.

Costas Vassiliou (1939), with sarcasm and expressive boldness, is sharply critical in his collections *Porphyras* (1978) and The *Annunciation of Lygeri* (1988). Through a personal mythology, the poetic discourse of Vassiliou expresses the recent tragedy in a singular harsh lyric tone, while the unvarnished view of contemporary Cypriot reality is characterised by intense non-conformity. The poet chooses mainly biblical rhetoric, as has been noted by the critics, to project the machinery of alienation and de-Hellenisation in a denunciatory manner. A particularly interesting aspect of his work is the development of the persona of Rimacho. In other collections also, *Pieta* (1987) and *Lambousa* (1996), the poetic discourse deviates into the political accusation of whatever contributed to the overturning of the "World of Cyprus". In his last collections, in the Cypriot dialect, he attempts to elevate the vernacular into the space of poetry.

Pitsa Galazi (1940) expresses most frequently in poems of many lines the frustration of the generation who experienced the anti-colonial uprising of 1955-59. The difficulties of adapting to a world removed from this climate leads her to a continuous poetic

focusing on occupied Famagusta, lays bare the tragedy of Cyprus with realistic description. In *Metahistory* (1995), too, turning Cavafy and Seferis to fruitful use, the mature and pregnant poetic discourse

267

recreation of that period, particularly in the collections *Alexander's Sister* (1973), *Sleeplearning* (1978) and *Signallers* (1983). The memory operates in a dramatic way and the figures of the dead return expressively while the modernistic writing, with surrealist influences, merges a bitter lyricism, with plethoric discourse. In the poetic compositions *The Handsome Arthur or Arthur Rimbaud in Cyprus* (1991) and *The Birds of Efstathios and the Enclaved One* (1998) the political-historical and critical glance at the native space dominates.

Theoclis Kouyialis (1936). In the collection *Secret Burdens* (1971) the poetic discourse combines tender lyricism with human anguish. Later, in *Mythologion* (1981), his poetry is enriched both in expression and theme, with references to Leontios Makhairas and Pantelis Mechanikos, and turns critically, in satirical mood, to contemporary problems through mythmaking with a clear satirical element. In the collection *My Deftera* (1989) a swing to realistic writing is observed, projecting the human geography of his native space.

Michalis Pashiardis (1941) is a special case in the realm of Cypriot literature. He composes remarkable lyrical poetry. The spontaneous poetic vibration and an idiosyncrasy that is sensitive and sincere is diffused in his verses which stand out for their genuine inspiration. With *Dimensions* (1972) he enriches his poetry as regards themes and expression and converses fruitfully with poets such as Nikiforos Vrettakos, Tassos Leivaditis, Yiannis Ritsos et al. The historical events in Greece and on the island

are described in quite a number of the poems in the collection. The tragic experience of Cyprus lends a dramatic tone to his poetry in the collections *The Road of Poetry II* (1976) and *The Road of Poetry III* (1977). In his more recent collections, poems of a few lines predominate, a poetry of epigrammatic lyrical euphoria. Pashiardis has published quite a number of poems in the Cypriot vernacular which are characterised by an immediacy of expression.

Giorgos Philippou Pierides (1904-1999) lived till 1947 in Egypt and then in Cyprus, where he organised and directed, inter alia, the Famagusta Municipal Library. Four books of short stories which were published in the fifteen-year period 1963-1978 and which are characterised by firm writing, describe in a realistic manner the whole range of the historical-political and social reality on the island from the latter years of British rule till the Turkish invasion and its tragic consequences. *Tales of Difficulty* (1963), where the element of death emphasises dramatically the contradictions of the years of the anti-colonial liberation struggle, and *Times Immovable* (1966), where the picture is given of the closed urban society in the final years of colonial rule, portray the social environment in the years of British occupation. *Times of Affluence* contains short stories from penultimate Cyprus (1975) which are the prose of a mature creator. With a plain style and narrative immediacy, he records daily life through a description of urban life in which the social climate appears vividly. The personae and the setting depict the closed urban society on the island. The affluence and the dreadful daily routine of the heroes make up the picture of a world enclaved

G. PHILIPPOU PIERIDES

TETRALOGY OF THE TIMES

STORIES OF CYPRUS

TRANSLATED FROM GREEK BY
DONALD E. MARTIN AND SOTERIOS G. STAVROU
WITH A PREFACE BY THEOFANIS G. STAVROU

in the already looming tragedy. The subject matter is drawn from the contemporary reality of a static world where the political and social transformations do not leave scope for escape to real changes. *Times of Suffering* (1978) records the consequences of the coup d'état and the Turkish invasion.

Another prose writer, Theodoros Marsellos (1907-1991), known for The *Golden Mountains* (1947) and the novella *The Verger* (1958), gave in his later short stories the sense of the fleeting and a particular and unique psychological ability to penetrate (*The Thief in my House*, 1974). The unexpected and the inner world of the heroes are given in the novella *Utopia* (1981).

Ivi Meleagrou (1928) will give with her prose work the picture of contemporary Cyprus, making fruitful use of contemporary narrative technique. In the collection of short stories *Anonymous City* (1963) the modernistic writing presages her novels. The crossing of the tragic events of the history of the island, the climate of euphoria and the fragile course of the Cyprus problem will go on to lend a singular historicity to these works. The atmosphere of post-independence Cyprus from the summer of 1963 till the intercommunal clashes in December the same year, are given very convincingly in the novel *Eastern Mediterranean* (1969) and the narrative inventiveness is composed of flowing language. In *Penultimate Era* (1981) Meleagrou dissects Cypriot society with dramatic tone. The atmosphere shortly before the coup d'état and the political instability in the early years of the Republic of Cyprus are recast into literary material with innovative narrative techniques. *Penultimate Era* is a novel which stands out for the originality of its structure and narration and at the same time, with its political vividness, it is also a warning.

Ivi Meleagrou

Lina Solomonidou (1924-2008), who had appeared in 1959-60 with two short stories under the pen-

Lina Solomonidou

name of Aliki Lemezi, describes in her prose work with narrative immediacy views of contemporary life, projecting aspects of recent Cypriot history. The years of the anti-colonial liberation struggle are recast in the novel *Here Lies* (1964). *The Journey* (1969), with its singular writing and modern manner of expression, is written with vigour and tension and projects the blind alley of flight of the people. In her last book, *Cyprus – Experiences 1974* (1977), a unique, revealing testimony as Roger Milliex noted, the tragedy of Cyprus is depicted spherically through personal interviews of the people who lived through the events of 1974, as well as notes of the author and clippings from newspapers.

Christakis Georghiou (1929) in two collections of short stories (*Parallels*, 1964 and *Cracks*, 1970) records realistically aspects of later colonial rule, the intercommunal clashes and, in short stories of the later collection, the existential impasses. With the novel *Hours 1950* (1980) the general atmosphere of the last years of British rule is graphically presented through the Nicosia prison, while in *Archipelago* (1990) the historical-social environment of the last years of British rule and the first years of the Republic of Cyprus is described.

Andis Hadjiadamos (1936-1990) creates in his work a utopian world where everything, animate and inanimate, moves in the space of the absurd, the unexpected and the irrational with singular and non-conformist writing. The prose narrative in *Sknipoyiak* (1982) and *Krepello* (1987) presents the dream world of the author with subversive image-making, rich nomenclature and its connotations and

the surrealistic origin of this disguise. With his third book *Zanzouera* (1990), with verse and prose texts written for the most part in the Cypriot vernacular, the absurd aspect of life and the satirical projection of social pathology are described with renewed fun and linguistic overturnings.

Yiannis Katsouris (1935-2010) moves in a realistic climate in his first two collections of short stories, *Three Hours* (1966) and *The Fixed Point* (1973); contemporary life and its impasses appear with satire and humour in his work. The collection of short stories *Give us Today* (1979) is a remarkable testimony of the coup d'état and Turkey's 1974 military invasion. With sarcastic mood and expressive power he describes the context of the period. In his novel *Ascent of Stylianou* (1990), which gains effectiveness by suggestiveness, he records the historicalsocial reality in the years

Yiannis Katsouris

of the Second World War up to the inter-communal clashes of 1963 in a demystifying way, using humour and irony. Other novels by Katsouris are *Dear Uncle Michael* (2001), in which he describes in a demystified way, the adventures of the main hero, and *According to Evagoras and Evgenia or the Struggles of the Cuckold* (2009).

Panos Ioannides (1935) in his collection *Cypriot Epics* (1979) depicts the society of the first years of the Republic of Cyprus, frequently with sarcasm and irony. The war and the post-war period are portrayed

with firm technique in the collection of stories *The Unseen Aspect* (1979). In the book *Nicolas Kay, Journalist: True Parables* (1988) he debunks the complacency of a world which is tottering in the midst of frivolity and eudemonism. And in his novel *The Unbearable Patriotism of P.F.K.* (1989), which is set in the first years after the Turkish invasion in 1974, the sarcasm reaches its peak at the reception near the Green Line that divides the capital city of Nicosia. The complacency, the grotesqueness and the proposed solution of the Cyprus problem compose a thoroughly comic human geography with clear and accurate criticism of an alienated world which does not want or cannot take on its responsibilities.

Rina Katselli (1938) in the chronicle-testimony *Refugee in my Own Land* (1975) records her painful experience of the 1974 Turkish invasion in direct discourse, while in the novel *The Blue Whale* (1978) she expresses, with the original myth and the symbolic extensions, the anguish for Cyprus and its people. She is an author of many works at the centre of which lies her birthplace Kyrenia, now occupied by the Turkish army.

* * *

Author's note:
In a short article omissions are a problem, especially of people who contributed to the elevation of literature: Nikos Kranidiotis, Kypros Chrysanthis, Costas Proussis, Andreas Christofides and others. Also the absence of younger writers, mainly poets, and of prose writers, is a gap in this review of the literature of Cyprus.

TURKISH CYPRIOT LITERATURE
Gurgenc Korkmazel

THE 1960s
The euphoria of the declaration of the Republic of Cyprus in 1960 did not last long. The break-out of conflict between the two communites, naturally did not do any favours to Turkish Cypriot Literature. However, the production of poetry continued much more so than the short story or the novel.

In the mid-1960s, with the influence of the *Ikinci Yeni* in Turkey, a new movement began in Cyprus which is called *Soyut Şiir* (Absract Poetry). Innovators of this movement were Kaya Çanca, Fikret Demirağ and Mehmet Kansu. These poets and writers, and others of the same generation (Süleyman Uluçamgil, Orbay Deliceırmak and Numan Ali Levent), complained that not enough written heritage had been left to them. (There were sources in the Ottoman language, but they could not read them. Also, because literature produced before them was influenced to a great degree by Turkish Literature produced in Turkey, they did not see it as an important heritage). Therefore, they tried to create this tradition (heritage) for themselves. They did everything with this in mind.

Kaya Çanca, perhaps the most original voice of his generation, published in the 1960s, before his death, his only two poetry books: *Eski Beste*, 1965 and *Y.Sokağı,* 1968.

> In the mid-1960s, with the influence of the Ikinci Yeni in Turkey, a new movement began in Cyprus which is called Soyut Siir (Absract Poetry).

Fikret Demirağ

Also Taner Baybars (1936-2010), published his first poetry book in Turkish, but consequently settled in England, and from 1963 wrote his poems and novels in English.

During these years, the most well-known writers, as far as quality and productivity is concerned, were: Özker Yaşın and Fikret Demirağ. Later, Özker Yaşın chose to write ultra nationalist books. Fikret Demirağ, however, preserved his conciliatory stance and never created his poetry from the materials of the war.

Again, in these years, important names were Hikmet Afif Mapolar (1919-1989) who since the 1930s published short-stories and novels; and Numan Ali Levent (1935-2001), playwright and short story writer.

Poets and writers like Gür Genç, Faize Özdemirciler, Jenan Selçuk and **Ridvan Arifoğlu**, who belong to the generation of the 1990s continue to 'reject' nationalism and militarism. Their poetry is more provocative, atheist, anarchrist, and against the establishment.

The 1970s

Great social changes, like the continuation of conflict, enclaves, troops from Turkey landing on the island in 1974, the wave of migration and other reasons gave a new direction to Turkish Cypriot Literature.

Ironically, while these changes were happening on the island, 'Toplumcu Şiir' (Socialist Poetry) again, which was over in Turkey, came to Cyprus. The most successful name of 'Toplumcu Şiir' is Fikret Demirağ, who in the 1970s, published two important poetry books: *Ötme Keklik Ölürüm* (1972) and *Dayan Yüreğim* (1974). Besides him, another productive poet during these years is Osman Türkay, writing both in Turkish and English.

In the 1970s, leaving aside Fikret Demirağ, Mehmet Kansu and Zeki Ali, who published his first poetry book (*Bayan Mavi*, 1970), and Kaya Çanca (who committed suicide in 1973), almost all the Turkish Cypriot poets and writers living in Cyprus, wrote in a nationalist tone.

The 1980s

The 'Generation of 1974' or 'Rejection Front' which was formed by Mehmet Yaşın, Neşe Yaşın, Hakkı Yücel and Filiz Naldöven: Apart from the fact that they were against nationalism and militarism, it was the first time in Turkish Cypriot literature that a generation began to hold up the Cypriot identity in their speech and writing, and refer to Cyprus itself as their homeland, instead of Turkey. In this way, it is the first time that a movement came not from Turkey but began within Cyprus.

Fikret Demirağ, adjusting his poetry to all these changes, is also influenced by this movement. In his new poetry he makes more intense use of the ancient history and mythology of Cyprus.

Özden Selenge, who in her short stories and novels writes about the disappearance of rural life and traditional values, publishes her first short-story book: *Çiçeklenmeliyiz Biz Erik Ağacı* (1987). Also, Feriha Altıok, Ümit Inatçi and Tamer Öncül, publish their first poetry books in the 1980s.

The 1990s

Poets and writers like Gür Genç, Faize Özdemirciler, Jenan Selçuk and Ridvan Arifoğlu, who belong to the generation of the 1990s continue to 'reject' nationalism and militarism. Their poetry is more

provocative, atheist, anarchist, and against the establishment. And, contrary to the identity crisis and traumatic writing of the 'Rejection Front', they bring a new perspective of multi-identity and humour to Turkish Cypriot literature. Also, they accept as part of their heritage, some poets/writers who were denied by the 'Rejection Front'. Especially, Gür Genç and Jenan Selçuk, use sexuality in their writing, sometimes to the degree of pornography.

In the mid-1990s Mehmet Yaşın and Derviş Zaim publish their first novels in Istanbul and both of them are awarded prizes.

2000-2010/ Conclusion
Since the beginning, in all periods, Cypriot Turks have produced more poetry than any other kind of literature.

We can say that especially during the last fifty years, we see more island and Mediterranean culture in Turkish Cypriot literature. Probably, this is the main difference from Turkish literature in Turkey, generally, and it is a common base between Greek and Turkish Cypriot literature.

In these years, Emre Ileri and Senem Gökel in poetry, Mehmet Arap in the short story and Cengiz Erdem in novel, who in three years has published three philosophical novels, can be named as the most promising newcomers.

By way of conclusion, I offer a quotation from Fikret Demirağ: "On this small island of the East Mediterranean, there is a Turkish poetry, which is finally free from the centre, which has formed its own 'island' and began to connect to the poetry of the world!"

STATE PRIZES FOR LITERATURE
Maria Thoma

The State Prizes for Literature were launched in 1968 and have operated continuously for forty-two years now, indicating the quality standards of literary production on the Island. Prize winning books must be the kind that contribute to the development and evolution of each genre in Greek literature.

The institution of the State Literary Prizes initially included only the categories of Poetry and Prose, but soon the categories of Essay and Prize for Young Writer were added. Later on, prose was split into Prize for Novel and Prize for Short Story. From 1969 until 1992, the State Prizes for Literature also included the Prize for Overall Achievement. Andis Pernaris, Costas Montis, Pavlos Liassidis, Xanthos Lissiotis, Andreas Georgiadis-Kiproleon, Giorgos Philippou Pieridis, Yiannis Stavrinos-Economidis, Kypros Chrysanthis, Nikos Kranidiotis and Costas Proussis were the writers who received this prize. Apart from the Prize for Overall Achievement during the past forty-one years more than two hundred books in all other categories have received a State Prize for Literature.

In 2010, the State Prize for Literature categories are: Poetry, Novel, Short Story, Essay / Study, Chronicle/ Testimony, Study on the Literature and Culture of Cyprus by a non-Cypriot writer (every three years),

Prize for Debut Writer, Literary Work in the Cypriot Dialect (every three years). Parallel to these, there are also the State Prizes for Children's or Teenagers' Literature and the State Prize for the Illustration for Children's or Teenagers' Books.

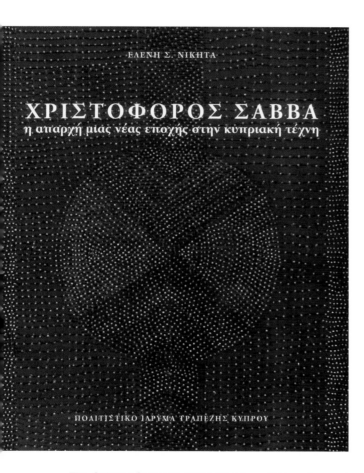

changes. Since 2009, the Ministry of Education and Culture has done away with the nomination process of books by the authors themselves. Instead, the institution now utilises the possibilities offered by the bibliographical system of the Cyprus Library (the Cyprus Republic's copyright library) in order to gather all the literary works that have been written by Cypriots, or that have been written by foreign researchers and scholars of Cypriot culture and literature each year. Thus, there is a more precise representation of the published production for the books competing for the State Prizes for Literature, than when any writer interested could submit his or her book to the Ministry.

The jury for the State Prizes for Literature comprises seven members, whereas both the jury for the State Prizes for Children's or Teenager's Literature and the jury for the State Prizes for the Illustration of Children's and Teenager's books have five members each. Since 2008, the institution has operated only with independent members – none of its jury members is a Cultural Services officer, as used to be the case in the past. Each jury achieves its full independence through a new regulation that allows the members to elect the President from amongst themselves.

The Cultural Services of the Ministry of Education and Culture are in continuous dialogue with organisations and citizens, in order to achieve a steady improvement of the institution, as well as to remain updated and in accordance with social, cultural and technological

THEATRE*

Dr Andri Constantinou

There are indications of theatrical activity in Cyprus in ancient times but there has been very little research into the theatre of that period. Four ancient theatres have survived. These theatres date back to the Hellenistic and Roman eras and are situated across the island, at Salamis, Soloi, Kourion and Pafos. A religious drama from the Byzantine period, called *The Cypriot Cycle of the Passion* has been preserved but it has no connection with a stage performance.

We have clear evidence of theatrical activity from the second half of the nineteenth century. During the last years of Ottoman rule, few and far between performances by Cypriot amateurs and Greek touring troupes took place. After 1878, when power was transferred to the British, the number of foreign companies visiting Cyprus increased, more amateur theatre groups were established as associations and there were quite a number of school performances of ancient drama. During the last decades of the nineteenth century the first examples of playwrighting appeared in modern Cyprus, mainly on historical subjects. The first landmark in the history of theatre in Cyprus was the completion in 1899 of the Papadopoulos Theatre in Nicosia, an impressive theatre building, by Cyprus standards, built on the model of large theatres in Europe. Unfortunately, the theatre was demolished at the end of the 1960s.

Dramatics were also developed at the beginning of the twentieth century by groups of Turkish Cypriots. Initially the Turkish Cypriot theatre was based on traditional Turkish theatre, i.e. performances such as Karagiozis and popular forms of impromptu comedy, but later followed models of the western theatre. The first modern work was staged in 1908 and was called *Vatan Yahut Silistre* [Homeland or Silistria] by Namik Kemal.

A milestone in the theatrical life of Cyprus was the *Pafitiki Epitheorisi* [Pafian Revue], staged in 1918 in the small town of Pafos by the pioneers Sotirakis and Kostas Markidis. It was clearly influenced by the Athenian revue. The production went on tour to other towns and two more versions were performed in the following years. These performances signalled the passage from non-artistic amateur theatre at national or charity events to theatre interested in art and entertainment, and in this specific case in satire. The Revue later flourished in Limassol and Larnaka, while

> In the years between the world wars, the theatre of labour associations and organisations left its mark, while in the 1940s and especially during World War II, Cypriot theatre began to acquire more professionalism.

The presentation of the Greek Cypriot theatre is based on research by the author and on the relevant bibliography. We refer to the Turkish Cypriot theatre in short parenthetical paragraphs, due to the fact that the sole bibliography in Greek consists of articles in the magazine Epi Skinis [On Stage] and chiefly in the Theatre Diary of 2009 of the Limassol Theatrical Course dedicated to the subject of the Turkish Cypriot Theatre. Relevant information was drawn from the article of Yasar Ersoy in the publication in question.

"The Suppliants" by Euripides, THOC production (1978).

277

"Don Camillo" by Giovanni Guareschi–Sotiris Pantatzis, OTHAC production (1965).

it was Nicosia's turn in 1938, with the Mousiki Skini Lefkosias [Nicosia Musical Stage].

In the years between the world wars, the theatre of labour associations and organisations left its mark, while in the 1940s and especially during World War II, Cypriot theatre began to acquire more professionalism. The theatre companies Lyriko [Lyric], Neo Lyriko [New Lyric], Enosi Kallitechnon [Artists' Union], Orpheas and Prometheas, with the collaboration of directors from Greece, such as Angelos Vazas, Adamantios Lemos and Kostis Michaelides, marked a short-lived climax and contributed decisively to the development of the theatre.

As far as playwrighting up to 1960 is concerned, not only poetic dramas but also realistic plays on social issues were written, whilst interesting examples of satire also exist. Other notable works include those of Evgenios Zinonos (*O Dikigoros* [The Lawyer]), Tefkros Anthias (*I Dimoprasia* [The Auction]) and Demetris Demetriades or Dorian (*O Apogonos* [The Descendant]). Reference should also be made to the plays of A.A. Georgiades-Kyproleontas (*Mia Nychta sto Hani* [A Night at the Inn]) and *I Zoi en Tafo* [Life in the Tomb]) and Loukis Akritas (*Omirioi* [Hostages]). However, the greater part of the plays written during the period between 1940 until 1974 consists of works in the Cypriot dialect on subjects derived from rural life.

Initially the Turkish Cypriot theatre was based on traditional Turkish theatre, i.e. performances such as Karagiozis and popular forms of impromptu comedy, but later followed models of the western theatre.

"Ach Moustafa" by Costas Montis, United Artists production, (1960).

One of the first examples of *ethography* is *I agapi tis Marikkous* [The Love of Marikkou] by Kyriakos Akathiotis (1938), performed many times by professional and amateur troupes.

Cypriot ethography often contains music and songs and the spectacle often includes traditional dances. The first example of this type of comedy is *To Oneiro tou Tzypri tou Lefkariti* [The Dream of Tzypris Lefkaritis] by Kostas Harakis with music and songs by Achilleas Lymbourides. With this performance in 1951, the Kypriako Theatro [Cypriot Theatre] embarked on its course and went on to develop rich activity until 1961. A key figure was the popular comedian Nikos Pantelides. In the 1950s Kypriaki Skini [Cypriot

"Glass Menagerie" by Tennessee Williams, ETHAL production (2009).

Stage] and Enomenoi Kallitechnes [United Artists] also appeared, led by Vladimiros Kafkarides, and there were also some performances of operas. These theatre companies were based in Nicosia while in Limassol groups of experienced amateurs enlivened the life of the theatre under the direction of Keimis Raftopoulos.

Plays in Turkish, including Turkish operetta, were produced during the 1920s and 1930s in the theatres of Beliğ Paşa, Papadopoulos and Magic Palace. During the 1930s and 1940s Turkish Cypriot athletic and rural organisations successfully developed theatre activity.

With Cyprus' independence, an impressively dynamic period ensued in theatre: many companies appeared and a multitude of productions was produced during each theatrical season. Professional theatre in Cyprus was established and began to mature. Artistic demands increased, a lot of actors pursued theatrical studies and almost all of them could make their living from acting. The companies which decisively contributed to the development of the theatre in Cyprus during the first years of independence were the Theatro Technis [Arts Theatre], the OTHAK [Organisation of Theatrical Development in Cyprus], the Theatro RIK [Theatre of the Cyprus Broadcasting Corporation (CyBC)] and the Peiramatiki Skini [Experimental Stage].

> In 1969, the Cyprus Broadcasting Corporation founded a theatre company that was known as the Theatraki tou RIK [Little Theatre of CyBC]. It was supported by personalities such as Andreas Christofides and Evis Gavrielides.

The Theatro Technis (1961-1962) was an effort to rejuvenate theatre by very young actors, including Nicos Charalambous and Stelios Kafkarides and the director Thanos Sakketas. OTHAC (1961-1968) began with ambitious plans and a demanding repertoire and was the first theatre group to receive a state subsidy. Its first director, Kostis Michaelides was followed by Yiorgos Filis. After 1964, OTHAC turned to revue, Greek farce and Cypriot ethography. In 1969, the Cyprus Broadcasting Corporation founded a theatre company that was known as the Theatraki tou RIK [Little Theatre of CyBC]. It was supported by personalities such as Andreas Christofides and Evis Gavrielides. Through the dynamism of those who inspired it, the homogeneity and the zeal of the team and its bold repertoire, the company introduced high artistic standards to the Cypriot theatre life. Jenny Gaitanopoulou and Despina Bebedeli made their mark as leading actresses at the Theatraki. The company broke up in 1971 following the foundation of the THOC [Cyprus Theatre Organisation]. A major contribution was made by the directors Nicos Shiafkalis and Vladimiros Kafkarides during the 1960s with the companies they founded and the performances they staged. Peiramatiki Skini [Experimental Stage] (1972-1974), founded by the young actors Costas Charalambides, Lenia Sorocou and Eftychios Poulaides left its imprint through productions of pioneering work in small spaces and an emphasis on the art of acting.

As regards playwrighting following Cyprus' Independence, plays referring to the recent

An exhibition of costumes and stage designs organised by the Cyprus Theatre Organisation in 2007.

281

Anticolomial struggle of 1955-59, such as *O Anaxios* [The Unworthy] by Rina Katseli, and previous periods of Cyprus' history started to appear. The main volume of plays was ethographical and mainly musical ethographical comedies. The most important representative of ethography was Michalis Pitsillidis, who introduces social issues in this tradition. A particular case was that of Michalis Pasiardis whose work moves on the fringes of ethography but is imbued with poetry. From independence up to the foundation of THOC in 1971, a plurality of writers produced work for pure entertainment, ethographical comedy, revue and political satire. Some examples include Demetris Papademetris, Marcos Georgiou, Achilleas Lymbourides, Sotos Oritis, Anthos Rodinis, Savvas Savvides, Michalis Kyriakides and Andreas Potamitis. Other playwrights also tested their abilities with different forms and subjects. Examples include the polymorphous work of Panos Ioannides and the polygraph Eirena Ioannidou-Adamidou.

> The Cyprus Theatre Organisation (THOC) was founded in 1971. It is remarkable that Cyprus acquired its state theatre just eleven years after the declaration of independence.

The Turkish Cypriot professional theatre company called *Ilk Sahne* [First Stage], was founded in February 1963. In 1965, First Stage enjoyed the subsidy of the Turkish Cypriot Communal Chamber and was renamed Turkish Cypriot First Stage Theatre. The theatre group attracted a regular and devoted public. In 1971 the troupe *Altun Sahne* [Golden Stage] was founded, which also performed plays in the Turkish Cypriot dialect, such as the play of Kemal Tunç *Alikko ile Caher*.

"Pluto" by Aristophanes, THOC production (2008).

The Cyprus Theatre Organisation (THOC) was founded in 1971. It is remarkable that Cyprus acquired its state theatre just eleven years after the declaration of independence. The first director of THOC was Nicos Chatziskos. In December 1972 the direction of THOC was taken over by Sokratis Karantinos, under the title of instructor-director. Karantinos supported THOC in its first steps with the confidence he showed in Cypriot directors and his devotion to the art of theatre. During its first three years, the Organisation shaped its identity despite the many difficulties faced, and consolidated itself. From 1972-1975 Iakovos Philippou served as managing director of the Organisation, while in 1975 Evis Gavrielides was appointed as its director, a position he held till the end of 1988.

"The Red Laterns" by Alecos Galanos, Theatro Ena production (2009).

In the years following 1974, the repertoire of THOC took on a political dimension. At the same time, THOC also gained prestige in Greece, mainly through the tours with Bertolt Brecht's *Mother Courage* in 1977, directed by Heinz Uwe Haus and Euripides' *The Suppliants* in 1979, directed by Nicos Charalambous. *The Suppliants* made an excellent impression and in 1980 was the first production of THOC at Epidaurus. The Organisation has participated to date with twenty-seven productions in the Festival of Ancient Drama of Epidaurus, with many successes to its credit, while Cypriot directors have made suggestions of their own with regard to the interpretation of ancient drama.

> At the end of the 1970s, theatrical groups began to make a dynamic appearance but were short-lived and at the end of the 1980s theatrical activity began to stabilise.

"*Laterna Ftohia kai Filotimo*", by Alecos Sakellarios, Satiriko Theatre production (2005).

In 1976 the Children's Stage of THOC produced its first play for children. In 1989 Andy Pargilly undertook the direction of the Organisation. Other directors include: Christos Siopachas (1995-1998), Andy Pargilly (1998-2007) and Varnavas Kyriazis (2007-). The New Stage of THOC was founded in the 1990s. The first attempts for the foundation of a second stage had already been made in 1976 with plays from the modern repertoire. The Experimental Stage was inaugurated in 2001, extending the repertoire of THOC and offering nowadays a space for alternative productions and new playwrights.

During the first years following the coup d'état and the Turkish invasion, theatrical activity in Cyprus dwindled to that of THOC and of groups performing revues. At the end of the 1970s, theatrical groups began to make a dynamic appearance but were short-lived and at the end of the 1980s theatrical activity began to stabilise. The enactment of subsidies, following the activation of the THOC Development Sector contributed to this. This activity began to shape Cyprus theatre in its current form. In 1986 members of the Kafkarides family and close collaborators founded the Satiriko Theatro [Satirical Theatre]. In 1987 Andreas Christodoulides founded Theatro Ena [Theatre One] and is still its director. In 1989 Limassol personalities founded the Limassol Theatre Development Company (ETHAL). Its Director today is Menas Tigkilis. A similar initiative took place in Larnaka in 1996 with the foundation of the Scala Theatre. Its director today is Andreas Melekis. The Anoictho Theatro [Open Theatre], Theatre Dionysos, Theatre Anemona [Anemone] in Nicosia, Theatre

Stage design and costumes exhibition organised by THOC, (2007).

"Matias the 1st", by Alki Zei,
ETHAL Children's Theatre (2007).

Versus in Limassol as well as a lot of other, mainly young groups operate today, without a permanent base, and occasionally offer pleasant surprises within the theatrical plurality and decentralisation.

As far as the theatrical activity of Turkish Cypriots is concerned, in 1975, the Turkish Cypriot Theatre First Scene was renamed Turkish Cypriot "State" theatre (Kibris Türk Devlet Tiyatrosu). In 1980, following their dismissal for political reasons, four artists (Yaşar Ersoy, Osman Alkaş, Erol Refikoğlu and Işın Cem) founded the Theatre of the Turkish Municipality of Nicosia (Lefkoşa Türk Belediye Tiyatrosu). The theatre company, renamed later on the Turkish Cypriot Municipal Theatre of Nicosia (Lefkoşa Belediye Tiyatrosu), extended the repertoire, undertook the organisation of various related activities (festivals etc.) and worked for the rapprochement of the two communities through collaborations with the Satiriko Theatre. In the 1980s and 1990s, mainly amateur groups were active, such as Theatre Emek in Famagusta, Theatre GÜSAD (Güzel Sanatlar Derneği), meaning Union of Fine Arts), the Private Artistic Company of Morfou and the Company of the Cyprus Chamber of Arts. The Turkish Cypriot Comedy Group attracted the interest of the public by presenting works in the Turkish Cypriot dialect. In the meantime, the Turkish Cypriot "State" Theatre, which was mainly staffed by artists from Turkey, changed its staffing policy and employed local artists as from 1994 an action that was positively viewed by the Turkish Cypriot press. From 2004 onwards it entered

> The Turkish Cypriot Comedy Group attracted the interest of the public by presenting works in the Turkish Cypriot dialect.

into an era of restructuring with an extended theatre company and increased productions every year.

After the coup d'état and the 1974 invasion, many Greek Cypriot playwrights tackled the shock, trauma and changes brought directly and indirectly to Cypriot society by this political blow. Examples include: Panos Ioannides and Rina Katselli from the older generation and Yiorgos Neofytou, Maria Avraamidou and Andreas Koukkides from the next generation. Examples of writers who appeared in the last fifteen years are Evridiki Pericleous-Papadopoulou, with plays that are poetic and Nearchos Ioannou, Antonis Georgiou and Adonis Florides, who attempt to broaden their subject matter with modern issues of Cypriot society.

"All About my Mother" by Samuel Adamson based on the film by Pedro Almodovar, Scala Theatre production (2010).

"Das kleine Mahagonni" by Brecht, ETHAL production (2009).

TRADITIONAL ARCHITECTURE
Irene Hadjisavva

The rich history of Cyprus, from the dawn of human civilisation to the end of the Middle Ages, is documented by significant monuments. But alongside the ancient ruins and the Byzantine churches lies the anonymous vernacular architecture, which forms the built environment of our historic settlements. The traditional buildings, constructed to shelter the life and aspirations of ordinary people, encapsulate the material expression, the living testimony of the culture, the beliefs and the social, political and economic circumstances of our ancestors.

> The church was the most important part of the historic core, a gathering place for the social and economic activity of the inhabitants.

The form and organisation of settlements and the vernacular buildings that create them depend on the topography of the land, the climatic conditions, the available materials and their properties, but also on socio-economic factors. The villages seem to organically grow into the landscape, whether that is part of steep mountains, rounded hills or plains, forming a remarkable unity of the natural and manmade environments. Settlements were compact, densely built, with narrow, earthen or stone-paved streets uniting the individual dwellings and tracing the way to the agricultural land in the outskirts. The church was the most important part of the historic core, a gathering place for the social and economic activity of the inhabitants. Other public spaces were rare, usually developed alongside the main road leading to the settlement.

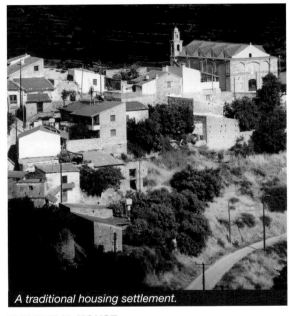

A traditional housing settlement.

THE RURAL HOUSE
The rural house was built by the local dwellers without following a set plan, but according to the needs of the family. The organisation of the house reflected the introverted nature of the community. The closed inner courtyard was the heart of the house, a main living and working space for both people and animals. Surrounded by high walls, it was an inherent and necessary component of the dwelling space and provided access to the different parts of the house. This was usually composed of two or three *makrinaria* (narrow long rooms), cellars and/or *dichora* (double space rooms) which were always positioned against

A mountain housing settlement.

the edges of the plot, either in a linear or in an L-shape formation. Access to the courtyard from the house was achieved via a courtyard door that led straight to it, or through a semi-opened arched portico. The rooms were rarely linked to each other and had doors usually only facing the courtyard. The *dichoro* was the most important internal space of the house. It had multiple functions; it served as living and sleeping room, reception space, but could also house the animals. It was formed by doubling the width of a *makrinari* by replacing the wall in between with a wooden beam spanning the whole length of the room, or by inserting a stone arch in the place of the dividing wall. When the arch was used, this room was called *palati* (palace).

> Access to the courtyard from the house was achieved via a courtyard door that led straight to it, or through a semi-opened arched portico. The rooms were rarely linked to each other and had doors usually only facing the courtyard.

The *iliakos* (sun-room) was another important feature of the traditional house. It was a semi-covered space, open on one side toward the courtyard facing the sun, by one or more consecutive arches or beams on poles, according to its length. It also provided access to the adjacent rooms of the house. In many cases the *iliakos* was repeated on the upper floor. These were the most interesting morphological features of the whole composition of the dwelling.

A second floor was built usually when the plot was small and did not allow for ground floor extensions. Access to the second floor rooms was always via an external stone or wooden staircase located in the courtyard against the front elevation of the main house and usually ending in a small covered wooden balcony. The doors and windows were small and few

A courtyard of a traditional house.

and proportioned according to the structural qualities of the building materials. Openings toward the street were scant, usually with only a front door and an *arsera* (a small window) high above it for ventilation. The houses were always positioned toward the south or the east to absorb as much sunlight as possible.

A restored courtyard of a traditional house.

The urban house.

> The individual rooms in a house were organised along a principle which was to become the nucleus for each urban housing unit.

On higher elevations on the mountains, the topography of the land limited the space available for housing. In this case a courtyard was rare and the buildings seem to be clambered on several levels on the steep slope. The different levels of the houses were accessed straight from the streets at different elevations. There was often an *iliakos*, this time on the highest level of the house, forming a kind of covered verandah.

THE URBAN HOUSE

The transition from the rural to the urban type of dwelling began toward the end of the nineteenth and the beginning of the twentieth century, almost coinciding with the end of the Ottoman era. It also coincided with the emergence of the Cypriot middle class, the result of socioeconomic restructuring that brought with it a new perception of social and economic practices. The forms of the buildings consequently began to alter. With the new practices, the main rooms of the dwelling were defined, organised and all built together, at the same time. The middle-class owner began to create his own dwelling space, suited to his own specific needs, but still borrowed from the basic layout of the rural dwelling (which had by then become unsuited to his lifestyle). For some time, various areas, such as the kitchen, washroom and laundry room, remained in separate units from the main building due to their diminished importance as spaces for social functions. The location of the main house at the far end of the building plot became outmoded. The new urban type of dwelling, projected as one finite unit, needed to be displayed so that it could acquire social status.

It was gradually brought forward toward the front of the building plot, bordering the street. The new style, dictated by modernisation, was the neoclassical style, whose morphological elements adorned city mansions but also influenced the humble buildings of the period, in both the urban and rural environment.

The individual rooms in a house were organised along a principle which was to become the nucleus for each urban housing unit. The central hallway or *iliakos* served as an entry space from the street, while one or two rooms *(makrinaria)* were located symmetrically on either side of it. If the width of the plot allowed, one of these makrinaria would become a *dichoro* by the use of an arch. Originally, the *iliakos* itself used to have an open arch toward the courtyard in the back which later was closed off with a door. Despite small changes, the *iliakos*, remained the main room of the house.

Later, the strict symmetry governing the layout of the house became more elastic. Serving as a central hallway, the *iliakos* continued to have the same ample proportions, but one of the side rooms became wider to accommodate important social functions and evolved into the salon. Other rooms became smaller. The final phase in the evolution of the urban dwelling was completed when the house included all its necessary spaces under one roof and became one individual free-standing unit, situated within an urban fabric of similar units. Inside the dwelling, the tripartite organisation of rooms in the layout continued to persist, but over time became subject to numerous alterations with a noticeable break-away from symmetry. One end of the *iliakos* could be

A restored traditional house.

separated down the middle with glazing, while often a verandah appeared in place of the iliakos at the back of the house. Despite variations, the whole building was gathered under a four-pitched tiled roof.

In the plan of the symmetrical house, balance was also reflected in its facade, with the front door placed at the center, flanked by a window on either side. In cases where the building was moved back from the street, a covered portico shaded the front entry. This was achieved by taking space from the front of the original iliakos. On other occasions a covered porch was added along the whole front of the house. Windows appeared on the side elevations of these free-standing houses, and the side elevations themselves acquired compositional importance.

> With the introduction of new technology, the industrialised, easy-to-use new materials and the modern way of life, traditional architecture was inevitably abandoned.

With the introduction of new technology, the industrialised, easy-to-use new materials and the modern way of life, traditional architecture was inevitably abandoned. Young architects, educated abroad, returned to Cyprus in the 1950s – 1960s, bringing with them the modern movement. During the years following the Cyprus independence, the urban landscape transformed according to the modern international style. The first tall buildings appear, while the buildings' morphology expressed the technological achievements of the construction industry: extended cantilever concrete roofs, prefabricated brises-soleils, reinforced concrete structural frames. A large number of public buildings, including schools, were constructed during this period as well as tourist infrastructure to accommodate the emerging tourist industry. The new style was also adopted for the residences of the

A modern addition on a traditional building.

urban society who adopted the modern way of life in all its manifestations.

Contemporary architecture and techniques replaced or altered the historic building stock to a great extent. After a long period of indifference during which vernacular architecture was synonymous with rural misery, traditional/historic architecture as well as the modern movement, is once again appreciated for its cultural heritage value. Both rural and urban historic settlements enjoy a growing interest for their rehabilitation and revitalisation. The government supports this trend by providing generous financial and other incentives for restoration and rehabilitation projects and by organising events aiming at making the public aware of on the value of traditional architecture.

A restored flour mill.

CINEMA
Eleni Christodoulidou

The cinematographic production in a small country like Cyprus had an inevitable late start and a rather slow development in its early years. The history of cinema in Cyprus began at the end of the 1940s, when the British colonial government started to train Cypriot film makers at the Colonial Film Unit. With the advent of Cypriot television in 1957, the first short-length films, mainly documentaries, began to be produced.

The pioneers of Cypriot cinema during the 1950s were George Lanitis, Ninos Fenek Mikellides, Renos Watson, Polys Georgakis and others who directed and produced short-length films. Some of these were: The Island of Aphrodite, Salamina, Botrys of Cyprus, Epikoinonia (Communication), To Heri (The Hand) and Rizes (Roots) by Nikos Lanitis and George Stivaros.

Feature-length films were produced much later in the 1960s. George Filis in 1963 directed a film depicting the traditional Cypriot wedding, *Agapes kai Kaimoi* (Love Affairs and Heartbreaks) in 1965, and soon after *To Telefteo Fili* (The Last Kiss), *1821, and Cyprus*. In 1969, George Katsouris and Costas Farmakas directed the comedy *O Paras o Maskaras* (Money the Clown).

During the late 1960s and early 1970s there was a richer crop of films. George Filis produced and directed *Gregoris Afxentiou, Etsi Prodothike I Kypros* (Cyprus' Betrayal), and the *Mega Document*. The cinematographic entrepreneur Diogenis Herodotou also started producing films: *Dakrya kai Diplopenies* (Tears and Strings), *I Diki tou Fitilla* (Fitillas' Trial), *I Apagogi tis Gogous* (Kidnapping Gogou), *O Firfiris stin Athena* (Firfiris visits Athens), *To Ftohopedo tis Kyprou* (The Cypriot Pauper), *Diakopes stin Kypro* (Holidaying in Cyprus) and *O Tragoudistis tis Kyprou* (The Cyprus Singer).

In the mid and late 1970s Costas Demetriou produced and directed a number of feature films: *Ta Hassamboulia* (Vendetta), *Skotoste ton Makario* (Order to kill Makarios) and *Gia Pion Na Vrexi* (For Whom Should it Rain).

In the 1980s the following feature films were produced: *O Avrianos Polemistis* (Tomorrow's Warrior) by Michalis Papas; *Trimithi, O Viasmos tis Afroditis* (The Rape of Aphrodite) by Andreas Pantzis, that won first prize at the Thessaloniki Film Festival in 1985; and, *Nekatomenoi Aerides* (Troubled Winds) by Yiannis Ioannou. In 1985 Christos Shopahas was awarded first prize at the Moscow Film Festival for his film *I Kathodos ton Enia* (The Descent of the Nine).

In the 1990s, film productions include: *To Ftero tis Migas* (The Wing of the Fly) by Christos Shopahas which won the prize for best direction at the Thessaloniki Film Festival in 1995. *I Sfagi tou Kokora* (The Slaughter of the Cock) by Andreas Pantzis a Cypriot-Greek-Bulgarian co-production, won the prize for direction at the Thessaloniki Film Festival in 1996 and it was nominated by Greece as its representative in the Oscar Awards for best foreign language film for

> The history of cinema in Cyprus began at the end of the 1940s, when the British colonial government started to train Cypriot film makers at the Colonial Film Unit.

"Akamas", directed by Panicos Chrysanthou (2006).

1997. In the same year, *Dromoi kai Portokalia* (Roads and Oranges) was produced by Aliki Danezi Knutsen. In 1999 there was *Vysinokipos* (Cherry Orchard), an adaptation of Chekhov's play by Cypriot-born director, Michael Kakoyiannis.

Cinematographic production in Cyprus received a boost in May 1994 with the establishment of the Cinema Advisory Committee. The Committee is mandated to recommend for funding the best proposals submitted by Cypriot producers/directors in the categories of feature-length films, short films, documentaries and animation.

Until now, the Cyprus government allocated financial support for more than 130 films. Currently, the annual funding budget is 1.500,000 euro.

Since 2003, the Ministry of Education and Culture is responsible for the Cinema Sector, through the "Programme for the Development of Cyprus Cinema" and its priorities are the cinematographic production, education and professional training. It finances international co-productions, high and low budget feature films, short films, documentaries, animation, experimental films, as well as the local distribution and circulation of Cypriot films in theatres. It also provides financial support for filmmakers to participate at international film festivals and markets and in various educational seminars and workshops abroad. Until now, the government allocated financial support for more than 130 films. Currently, the annual funding budget is 1.500,000 euro.

More recent feature-film productions include: *Kai to Treno Paei ston Ourano* (And the Train Goes to the Sky) by Ioannis Ioannou (2000); *The Road to Ithaca* by Costas Demetriou; *To Tama* (The Promise) by

"The Last Homecoming", directed by Corinna Avraamidou (2008).

"Honey and Wine", directed by Marinos Kartikkis (2006).

Andreas Pantzis; *Kato Apo ta Astra* (Under the stars) by Christos Georgiou; *Bar* by Aliki Danezi-Knusten (all in 2001); *Kokkini Pempti* (Red Thursday) by Christos Siopachas (2003); *Kalabush* by Adonis Florides and Theodoros Nikolaides (2003); *Me ti Psychi sto Stoma* (Soul Kicking) by Yiannis Economides (2006); *Meli ke Krasi* (Honey and Wine) by Marinos Kartikkis (2006); *Akamas* by Panicos Chrysanthou (2006); *Hi I'm Erica* by Ioannis Ioannou (2008); *O Teleutaios Gyrismos* (The Last Homecoming) by Corinna Avraamidou (2008); and, *Guilt* by Vassilis Mazomenos (2009). Currently, in 2010, there are three films in post-production: *Apo Thauma* (By a Miracle) by Marinos Kartikkis; *Deipno me tis Adelfes mou* (Dinner with my Sisters) by Michael Hapeshis; and, *Maxairovgaltis* (Knifer) by Yiannis Economides.

cinema

Kalabush
no work
no money
no love
a film by Adonis Florides & Theodoros Nikolaides

"Kalabush", directed by Adonis Florides & Theodoros Nikolaides (2003).

"Slaughter of the Cock" by Andreas Pantzis, prize for direction Salonica Film Festival (1996).

The Ministry of Education and Culture is also responsible for bilateral agreements and the promotion of Cyprus as a filming destination. Tax incentives are being promoted in collaboration with the Ministry of Commerce, Industry and Tourism. Cyprus is a member of Eurimage, the Media Programme, the SEE Cinema Network, the EFAD (European Film Agency Directors) and the EFARN (European Film Agency Research Network) and has signed the European Convention on Cinematographic Co-productions.

> The Ministry of Education and Culture is also responsible for bilateral agreements and the promotion of Cyprus as a filming destination.

Moreover, the Cultural Services section of the Ministry of Education and Culture, organises, on regular basis and in cooperation with other organisations, film festivals all around the year including: the "Mini International Festival: Cyprus Film Days"; the "Alternative Cinema Festival"; the "European Film Academy Shorts"; the "Cyprus Shorts and Documentaries Festival"; two documentary festivals; the "International Children's Film Festival"; and, screenings of various Cypriot films in rural areas. It also supports film clubs and associations like "The Friends of Cinema Society" and "The Directors Guild of Cyprus".

"The Road to Ithaca", directed by Costas Demetriou (2000).

*"The Last Homecoming",
directed by Corinna
Avraamidou (2008).*

MUSIC

Dr Elena Theodoulou-Charalambous

Music as an art innate in humankind may be associated with the visions, socio-political struggles, the historical course and the self-awareness of a people. Through this perspective music appears as a dynamic and composite phenomenon which "potentially" absorbs all the influences and effects of cultural co-existence and interaction of people, thus nurturing the promotion of cultural specificity, diversity and intercultural dialogue.

The Music of Cyprus, a free highlight in the intercultural vastness ...

Due to its unrivalled geopolitical and strategic position, Cyprus was subject to a number of conquerors and came under the influence of many foreign cultures and civilisations, something which is reflected in the musical tradition of the country. Indeed, in the music of Cyprus, ancient and primordial sounds meet within the lyrical intensity and depth; thus, the island's musical wealth incorporates elements and influences from the island's centuries-long and turbulent history as well as the Mediterranean temperament and collective identity. As it appears through various historical sources and writings, from antiquity, the musical influence of mainland Greece was not only obvious but also of substantial significance. As Plutarch notes, the kings of Cyprus sponsored the organisation of musical contests of circular dances and songs with actors and singers whom they brought from mainland Greece[1]. Moreover, from the representations on the various vases and from other historical sources, it appears that both in Cyprus and in the mainland Greek space the same musical instruments were used. Another very characteristic element was the fact that music was indissolubly interwoven with all aspects and manifestations of both private and public life[2].

Apart from the above musical influences, one can discern in the musical wealth of the island the existence of elements that refer to the space of the wider Mediterranean basin; in most cases, indeed, these influences concern some musical "borrowing back" of ancient Greek music[3].

In the Medieval period, even though the existing sources on musical life in Cyprus are not many, there are, nonetheless, two very important works which give us valuable information. The one is a major work by Guillaume de Machaut (La Prise d'Alexandrie)[4] and the other is the "Manuscript of Cyprus" of the fifteenth century (Manuscript Torino J.ii.9)[5] which is

Manuscript Torino J.II.9., from the National Library of Turin.

[1] Plutarch, Moralia, 334E

[2] K.P. Hadjioannou, Ancient Cyprus in Greek Sources, Vol.I, Nicosia 1971.

[3] Beaton R. (1980) "Modes and Roads: Factors of change and continuity in Greek musical tradition", Annual of the British School at Athens, 75:1-11

[4] Palmer, R.Barton (Transl) (2002) Introduction to La Prise d'Alexandrie (The Taking of Alexandria), by Guillaume de Machaut. New York: Routledge.

[5] LMI [Libreria Musicale Italiana] (ed.) (1999) Codice J.II.9 / The Codex J.II.9 Facsimile Edition. Printed in Italy.

The Limassol Mandolinata, with the founder and director G. Hourmouzios (1910).

considered to be a work of fundamental artistic worth and constitutes living evidence of the music which the Lusignan rulers of Cyprus were accustomed to present in their daily life. Moreover this work stands out for its uniqueness since no part of it appears in any other manuscript. The manuscript is in the National Library of Turin and was miraculously saved with very little damage from the fire which broke out in the library in 1904.

During the period of Ottoman rule, because of poverty and oppression, the island was cut off from the rest of Europe and thus the artistic and cultural currents of Europe did not have any effect in Cyprus. The main genres of music which appear in this period are Byzantine ecclesiastical music and the traditional folk music of Cyprus.

> From the end of the 1920s the first schools of music, conservatoires, made their appearance through which a more systematic approach to the dissemination of musical knowledge was attempted.

With the arrival of the British in Cyprus, the western European musical tradition began diffidently to gain ground. At the same time, a lot of other social, historical and political events such as the Russian Revolution, the Persecution of the Armenians by the Turks and the Asia Minor Catastrophe (Greco-Turkish War of 1919–1922), contributed to the further cultivation of European music. From the end of the first decade of the twentieth century, Cypriot music groups were already making their appearance and playing artistic music.

A special role in the musical development of the country was also played by the various bands which began to be created. It is also worthy of mention that during the conflict over the succession to the office of Archbishop (1900-1909) and the formation of two opposing political parties in support of the Bishops of Kition and Kyrenia respectively, each party created its own band and music movement to attract supporters.

During the same period the systematic study and performance of ecclesiastical music began. Among the pioneer teachers, Stylianos Hourmouzios was the one whose work as regards the interpretation of Byzantine music had an important influence all over Cyprus. From the start of the decade of the 1920s, a significant turn is observed to the systematic study, research and preservation of our Cypriot musical tradition by the most important researchers of the great wealth of traditional music: Theodoulos Kallinikos, who published his very well-known book "Cypriot Muse" in 1951, and Sozos Tompolis. In 1967 Sozos Tompolis' book "Cypriot Rhythms and Melodies" was awarded a prize by the Academy of Athens.

From the end of the 1920s the first schools of music, conservatoires, made their appearance through which a more systematic approach to the dissemination of musical knowledge was attempted.

Within the framework of the intense musical activity comes the projection of the work of important Cypriot composers who laid the foundations for the creation of classical music in Cyprus.

The Mozart Orchestra of Cyprus founded in 1938, with director Solonas Michaelides.

The Cyprus State Youth Orchestra.

Moreover, between 1920 and 1939 there appears a very dynamic and intense musical development, and the foundations and groundwork were laid for the subsequent promotion of artistic music in Cyprus with the staging of Cypriot musical productions including operas and oratorios. The intense musical activity of this period created the conditions and the preconditions for the formation of the first orchestras (the Bedelian Symphony Orchestra, the "Olympiakos" String Orchestra in 1934, the "Olympiakos" Symphony Orchestra in 1935 and the Mozart Orchestra in 1938). The Mozart Orchestra was an important nucleus of musical development till 1963.

Reference to another musical genre which began to appear at about 1920, the revue, also merits reference in this short account.

The first Cypriot orchestras which began to be created from the late 1920s are a worthy successor in the continuation of the orchestral musical tradition in the State Orchestra of Cyprus and the State Youth Orchestra which were founded in 1987. Throughout all these years, the State Orchestra of Cyprus has played an invaluable role in the cultural revival of the island. It has served not only the needs of the community but was at the same time an important factor in the creation of professional opportunities. Furthermore, it functioned as an incentive for talented young people who wished to pursue professional training and a career in music. The State Youth Orchestra, which from the beginning functioned within the framework of the State Orchestra of Cyprus, was a nursery for

> The State Youth Orchestra, which from the beginning functioned within the framework of the State Orchestra of Cyprus, was a nursery for the promotion of talented young musicians.

the promotion of talented young musicians. From its foundation, the State Orchestra of Cyprus functioned within the structure of the Ministry of Education and Culture. However, in accordance with a decision of the Council of Ministers, the operational status of the State Orchestra and the Youth Orchestra have changed since 1 January 2007. The State Orchestra of Cyprus has been turned into an independent organisation and renamed the "Symphony Orchestra of Cyprus".

Contemporary Cypriot musical creation is characterised by a variety of expression and styles. More specifically, it includes all the genres of music (contemporary classical, jazz, Greek entechnon songs, pop, rock and others). Influences from the international milieu as well as from the musical currents prevailing in the wider European area are evident. Because of its geopolitical position, Cyprus has been at the crossroads of civilisations, a fact which has affected and still affects the musical process. All the influences, currents and trends are assimilated creatively through the contemporary reality of the Cypriot temperament, thus making the music of Cyprus a free sounding highlight in the intercultural vastness....

The Cyprus Symphony Orchestra.

DANCE

Throughout the post-independence years and since its foundation the Cultural Services department of the Ministry of Education and Culture has encouraged and supported choreographers and dancers in their artistic creation, has provided opportunities for education and further training at home and abroad, and has promoted and enhanced education opportunities in ballet as well as modern dance for children and youth. It has also provided opportunities for artists to perform their choreographic works in Cyprus and abroad.

These goals are achieved through various programmes which include, amongst others, subsidising of individual artists, dance groups and organised associations of professionals in the field of dance in Cyprus and the organisation of annual festivals, institutions and competitions where artists can present their work and perform in front of large audiences.

One of the most successful institutions in the field of dance is the Cyprus Dance Platform which was launched in 2001 and since then has hosted a plethora of dance works created by Cypriot choreographers and performed by individual Cypriot dancers or dance groups, varying from experimental to theatrical and contemporary dance. Lectures, workshops and round table discussions on issues of modern dance are also organised every year in the framework of the Platform.

Dance Platform.

The "Amphidromo Dance Company";
contemporary dance by Elena Christodoulidou.

"If not for you" by Arianna Economou, ECHO ARTS.

"Twitter" solo by Arianna Economou.

Sama dance group.

Furthermore, the Cultural Services initiated in 1998 the organisation of the European Dance Festival with the collaboration of the embassies and the cultural centres of the countries of the European Union. Following the accession of Cyprus to the EU in 2004 and the enlargement of the European family, the Festival has become an authentic celebration of European contemporary dance, enriching in this way the cultural life of the island and providing the opportunity to Cypriot artistes to become acquainted with their European colleagues and their work.

ECHO ARTS,
contemporary dance by
Arianna Economou.

INTERNATIONAL FESTIVALS

"KYPRIA"

Since its establishment in 1991, the "Kypria" International Festival has been the most important annual cultural event in Cyprus. The festival, held in all major cities in the government-controlled areas, features events in all fields of the performing arts. The festival hosts artists and ensembles of international acclaim from Cyprus, Greece and other countries and includes all forms of art, music, dance and theatre.

Since its initiation, the Ministry of Education and Culture has supported the event wholeheartedly and has spared no effort to include events of high cultural standards whilst also mediating for the promotion of intercultural dialogue.

The "Martha Graham Dance Company" of New York, Kypria Festival (2008).

"Party Animals",
Kypria Festival (2009).

313

PAFOS FESTIVAL

The Pafos Festival, officially launched in 1998, was the result of a joint effort between various professional bodies in Pafos with the aim of promoting the island's western town as an international centre of high-profile cultural events. A highlight of the cultural calendar not only for the coastal town but for the island as a whole, the opera festival has developed into an annual celebration.

The performances are set against the backdrop of the Pafos Castle and the area around the attractive harbour is converted into a stunning operatic arena.

The Pafos Aphrodite Festival aspires to offer all music aficionados a unique experience leading them through the magic paths of lyric drama.

"Lakme" by Leo Delibes, Sofia National Opera, Pafos Aphrodite Festival (2009).

"Nabucco" by Verdi, National Opera of Poland, Pafos Aphrodite Festival (2001).

"La Traviata" by Verdi, the National Opera of Poland, Pafos Aphrodite Festival (2005).

315

EUROPEAN DANCE FESTIVAL

The European Dance Festival is a very important international dance meeting with the participation of many European countries. A feast of contemporary dance meets all the trends, the dynamics and the new forms of the international contemporary scene through the works of representative groups of each country.

The increased level of participation by EU member states with performances and workshops is a clear indication that the Dance Festival is becoming an annual highlight of the European arts and culture scene.

The European Dance Festival was celebrated for the thirteenth consecutive year in 2010 in Cyprus. It is jointly organised by the Cultural Services Department of the Ministry of Education and Culture and the RIALTO Theatre in Limassol with the collaboration of the Embassies of the member-states of the European Union in Cyprus.

The 2010 European Dance Festival is dedicated to the fiftieth anniversary of the independence of the Republic of Cyprus. The participation of each country in the Festival will be considered as part of the official contribution of each member-state in the celebrations for the anniversary.

> The 2010 European Dance Festival is dedicated to the fiftieth anniversary of the independence of the Republic of Cyprus.

"Ajax" by Sophocles, Attis Theatre of Greece, Ancient Greek Drama Festival (2008).

ANCIENT DRAMA FESTIVAL

The Ancient Drama Festival is organised annually by the Cyprus Centre of International Theatre Institute, the Cultural Services and the Cyprus Tourism Organisation. It began in 1996 and is an annual event which attracts professional theatre companies from various parts of the world. It has hosted companies from Greece, Britain, USA, Germany, Russia, Romania, Sweden, Croatia, Bulgaria, Italy, Austria, Korea and Cyprus. This wide international participation in the Festival helps to bring out the universality of ancient Greek drama and underline its living presence in today's world. The Festival is held in July and early August when Cyprus attracts visitors from all over the world. Thus, with its performances it brings ancient Greek drama closer to a multicultural audience. The performances take place at various venues around Cyprus including the ancient amphitheatre at Kourion, the Pafos Ancient Odeon and the Makarios III Amphitheatre in Nicosia.

"Clouds" by Aristophanes,
Ancient Greek Drama
Festival (2009).

317

MUSEUMS

The museums in Cyprus contain exhibits representing the history of the island and include ceramics, sculpture, metal objects, jewellery, tomb groups, inscriptions as well as objects of traditional arts and crafts. The Department of Antiquities is responsible for maintaining the museums of the island and developing or creating new ones. The largest museum is the Cyprus Museum in Nicosia while each district has its own museum. Various smaller local or thematic museums were established at Kourion, (Episkopi), Kouklia (Palaipafos) Maa-Palaeokastro, Marion Arsinoe at Polis Chrysochous and recently at Idalion. The Medieval Museum is housed in the Castle of Limassol and small folk museums were established at Fikardou, Yeroskipou and Pano Lefkara (Museum of Traditional Embroidery and Silversmithing). The museums of Cyprus participate in many exhibitions around the world by loaning objects related to the themes of the exhibitions. Much interest is shown in the archaeology of Cyprus by many scholars who visit the island to study its monuments and antiquities. Also many exhibitions, symposia/conferences on the archaeology of Cyprus are organised every year abroad or in Cyprus in which members of the staff of the Department of Antiquities participate.

> Much interest is shown in the archaeology of Cyprus by many scholars who visit the island to study its monuments and antiquities.

THE CYPRUS MUSEUM
The Cyprus Museum in Nicosia is the largest archaeological museum in Cyprus. Work on the building commenced in 1908 was completed in 1924

The exhibition "Angelos Makrides - Fanos Kyriakou/ Synergy" at the Cyprus Museum (2009).

when Cyprus was still a British colony. The collections of the museum cover the Neolithic age to the Early Byzantine period (7th century AD). The collections consist of pottery, jewellery, sculpture, coins, copper objects and other artifacts exhibited in chronological order in various museum galleries.

Exhibits at the Cyprus Museum, Nicosia.

THE HOUSE OF HADJIGEORGAKIS KORNESIOS – ETHNOLOGICAL MUSEUM

The House of Hadjigeorgakis Kornesios in Nicosia was restored to house a small ethnological collection, a project which received a Europa Nostra award in 1988. This manor house is one of the most important surviving eighteenth century buildings in Nicosia. It was once the residence of the Dragoman of Cyprus, Hadjigeorgakis Kornesios who was executed by the Ottomans in 1809. The office of the Dragoman was introduced in Cyprus at the Start of the Ottoman rule and was abolished in 1821 with the Greek War of Independence.

CYPRUS STATE GALLERY OF CONTEMPORARY ART

The Cyprus State Gallery of Contemporary Art houses on a permanent basis the Cyprus state collection of contemporary art, while periodically it hosts important exhibitions from abroad as well as retrospective exhibitions of the pioneers of Cyprus fine arts. A register of artists is kept at the State Gallery, which includes biographical material, as well as a collection with the characteristic features of their work and an archive of slides and photographs. There is also an Art Library enriched annually with significant publications on the various arts (Visual Art, Photography, Dance, Cinema).

THE PIERIDES ARCHAEOLOGICAL MUSEUM

One of the best landmarks of Larnaka is an old colonial wooden mansion situated in Zenon Kitieos Street, just off Democratias Square. Built in 1825, it belongs to the Pierides family, one of the best known families of the town. Nowadays it houses the

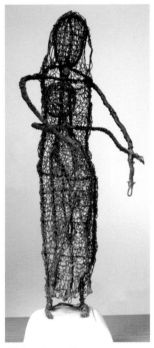

Christoforos Savva,
"Motherhood", 42x15,5x16cm
exhibited in the Cyprus State
Gallery of Contemporary Art.

The House of Hadjigeorgakis Kornesios, Nicosia.

Pierides Archaeological Collection, the outcome of a systematic acquisition of Cypriot antiquities by five consecutive generations in the family.

The founder was Demetrios Pierides (1811-1895), a scholar who studied literature in England. Upon his return to Cyprus he devoted his life to the protection of the historical treasures of his country. Using his wealth he would salvage discreetly archaeological treasures looted by tomb plunderers.

The last descendant of the Pierides family, Demetrios Z. Pierides, undertook its present arrangement and chronological classification. The collection has seen

Exhibits from the Pierides Museum, Larnaka.

additions of very rare pieces, especially pottery of the Early and Middle Bronze Ages, pottery of the Cypro-Archaic period, Cypro-Classical statues, Attic vases and some other new exceptional objects, including Chalcolithic Red-on-White pottery, pendants and picrolite idols (c. 3000BC).

Nowadays, the museum consists of four exhibit rooms to which, after the renovation of 1994, improved lighting and labelling were introduced as well as a small wing dedicated to medieval art plus assorted jewellery, embroidery and household utensils.

The Severis Gallery, Leventis Museum.

In 1989, the Municipality of Nicosia and the Anastasios G. Leventis Foundation opened the Leventis Museum to the public. The collections displayed in its permanent galleries represent over 5.000 years of the capital's history.

LEVENTIS MUSEUM
The Leventis Municipal Museum founded in 1984, presents the history and social development of the city of Nicosia from the Chalcolithic period (3.000 BC) to the present day. The Museum was founded in 1984 at the initiative of the then Mayor of Nicosia, Mr Lellos Demetriades.

The Museum is named after its donor, the Anastasios G. Leventis Foundation which bought and restored the building and which is administered by the Municipality of Nicosia.

In 1989, the Municipality of Nicosia and the Anastasios G. Leventis Foundation opened the Museum to the public. The collections displayed in its permanent galleries represent over 5.000 years of the capital's history. The collections are of a wide range and include archaeological finds, costumes, photographs, medieval pottery, maps and engravings, jewels and furniture.

The Artisans of Nicosia,
Leventis Museum, Nicosia.

Exhibits from the Kourion Archaeological Museum.

THE PANCYPRIAN GYMNASIUM MUSEUM

The Pancyprian Gymnasium Museum, situated in the historical centre of Nicosia, depicts the history of the oldest establishment of Secondary Education in Cyprus (founded in 1812) as well as many other aspects of Cypriot history and culture.

BYZANTINE MUSEUM

The Byzantine Museum contains the richest and most representative collection of Byzantine art in Cyprus. Over 200 icons dating from the ninth to the nineteenth century as well as ecclesiastical vessels, robes and books are exhibited in the museum. The sixth century mosaics from the church of Panagia Kanakaria in Lythrangomy are the most impressive of all the exhibits. These mosaics were returned to Cyprus after being illegally smuggled from the Turkish occupied part of the island.

FOLK ART MUSEUM

The largest and most important collection of Cyprus folk art can be found in the Cyprus Folk Art Museum in Nicosia set up in 1937. The collection belongs to the Society of Cypriot Studies and was put together by a group of pioneering Cypriot academics.

The historic building in which the Cyprus Folk Art Museum is housed was formerly the Archbishopric until 1960. The oldest building on the ground floor was part of a Gothic monastery of the fifteenth century with subsequent additions over the centuries.

The collection of the Cyprus Folk Art Museum includes select and representative examples of woven textiles, embroidery, costumes, wood carving, basketry, folk painting, miniatures and other articles from other branches of folk art from the whole of the island. The importance of this collection today is even greater because many of the ideas come from the Turkish occupied areas of Cyprus.

THALASSA MUSEUM

The Thalassa Ayia Napa Municipality Museum, under the direction of the Pierides Foundation and in association with the Hellenic Institute for the Preservation of Nautical Tradition, is a development of the Pierides Marine Life Museum founded in 1984. The museum's theme is the sea and it offers a pleasant scientific overview of the Cyprus marine life and sea treasures like fossilised fish, rare shells, corals, ceramics, engravings as well as replicas of famous vessels. The exhibits are displayed in four different sections and in the first section the visitor can trace the history of Cyprus by watching a film presenting a ship sailing through its different periods.

Exhibits from the Thalassa Museum, Agia Napa.

The Folk Art Museum, Nicosia.

UNESCO HERITAGE LIST

RESTORATION OF MONUMENTS

The restoration and conservation projects of ancient settlements, temples, theatres, castles, fortifications, churches/monasteries, mosques and houses of urban/rural traditional architecture are undertaken as well as the management plans of major archaeological sites (Nea Pafos and Choirokoitia) which have now been completed. The restoration of the Venetian Walls of Nicosia as a bicommunal project and funded by UNOPS, has also been completed.

> A relatively large number of monuments from Cyprus have been inscribed on the UNESCO World Heritage List.

A relatively large number of monuments from Cyprus have been inscribed on the UNESCO World Heritage List. In 1980 the archaeological sites of Kato Pafos and Palaipafos were inscribed, followed in 1985 by the inscription of nine painted churches of the Troodos regions, Panagia tis Forviotissa (Asinou), Agios Nikolaos Stegis (Kakopetria), Agios Ioannis Lampadistis (Kalopanagiotis), Panagia tou Araka (Lagoudera), Panagia (Moutoullas), Archangel (Pedoulas), Timios Stavros (Pelendri), Panagia Podithou (Galata) and Stavros tou Agiasmati (Platanistasa). The Neolithic village of Choirokoitia was inscribed in 1998 and the inscription of the nine painted churches was extended in 2001 to include the church of the Metamorphosis of Soter or Agia Sotira at Palaichori.

The fast pace of development in Cyprus and the increasing dangers to the preservation of the cultural

A wall-painting from the Church of Panagia Podithou in the village of Galata, inscribed on the UNESCO World Heritage List in 1985.

heritage has led to the expropriation of the most important archaeological sites so as to preserve them and to ensure the possibility of continuing scientific excavation and study in future.

In addition, efforts are being made for the preservation of the cultural heritage in the Turkish occupied part of the island where churches/monasteries, cemeteries and other monuments have suffered much destruction since 1974 as a result of looting or neglect.

The Church of Panagia Moutoulla inscribed on the UNESCO World Heritage List in 1985.

LEFKARA LACE

The traditional hand-made lace produced in the village of Lefkara, the reputed Lefkaritiko, was included in UNESCO's representative List of Intangible Cultural Heritage of Humanity on 30 September 2009.

Lefkaritiko lacemaking, this intricate form of needlework passed on from generation to generation, is among the seventy-six forms of expression added to the list by the twenty-four member-states of UNESCO's Intergovernmental Committee for the Safeguarding of Intangible Heritage during its fourth session in Abu Dhabi. The request for the inclusion was made by the Ministry of Education and Culture in co-operation with the Municipality of Lefkara.

> The tradition dates back to the Venetian period (1489-1571) when Venetian noble ladies used Lefkara as a retreat during the summer months to escape the heat of the lower plains, passing on their embroidery skills to locals.

The lace is now one of only two kinds of needlework included in the list, the other being Croatian. This particular lace making has been passed on from mother to daughter, and the young girls started to learn even before they went to school.

The tradition dates back to the Venetian period (1489-1571) when Venetian noble ladies used Lefkara as a retreat during the summer months to escape the heat of the lower plains, passing on their embroidery skills to locals. Nowadays, five centuries later, women of this 1.100 strong community still sit in doorways shaded with lush bougainvillea, nimbly working pieces of beige Irish linen with deft strokes of a needle and thread.

The Lefkaritika lace is included in UNESCO's Intangible Cultural Heritage List in 2009.

The UNESCO seal of approval will breathe new life into the craft. The Lefkara Municipality has already applied to UNESCO for funding its action plan seeking to preserve and expand this art, secure raw materials, assist the women who make the lace, help distribute their products and promote the Lefkaritiko at international exhibitions.

Lefkaritika lace-making in the village of Lefkara.

329

Traditional baskets.

HANDICRAFTS

The geographical position of Cyprus, at the crossroads of East and West, has contributed to the formation of a different kind of folk art and handicrafts.

Cyprus folk art has been influenced by successive conquerors. However, like the art of all eras of the island it absorbed foreign elements and has preserved its traditional character.

With the introduction of industrial technology, folk art retreated in stages, first from the towns and then, gradually, from the villages also and gave its place to mass production products which filled the Cyprus market.

> The main branches of traditional Cypriot folk art are weaving, embroidery, lace-making, pottery, wood-work, metal work, basket weaving and other smaller handicrafts.

The main handicraft centres of Cyprus were Nicosia, the Kyrenia district, especially the towns of Lapithos and Karavas, the Karpass peninsula, Akanthou, Morfou, the Messaoria area, Kilani village, Pafos and the Marathasa area.

One of the main reasons for the development of folk art and handicrafts is the abundance of raw materials such as cotton, flax, silk and wool for weaving and embroidery, pinewood and walnut trees for woodwork, clay earth for pottery and cane and wheat stems for basket weaving.

One of Cyprus' largest losses as a result of the military invasion by Turkey in 1974 was the destruction of the handicraft culture in the areas which are now occupied by Turkish troops. For this reason, the private as well as the public collections which are in the government-controlled areas of the island acquire special importance.

Especially rich in excellent examples of folk art is the Museum of Folk Art of the Cyprus Studies Company, which is housed in the former Archbishopric in Nicosia.

The main branches of traditional Cypriot folk art are weaving, embroidery, lace-making, pottery, wood-work, metal work, basket weaving and other smaller handicrafts.

Cypriot folk art is characterised by the primarily geometrical and severe designs, without, of course, lacking more freely patterned motifs from the plant and animal kingdoms, as well as themes from Hellenism and symbolic themes.

331

WINE TRADITION

The climate as well as the geographical position of Cyprus has contributed to making the island the birthplace of wine with the richest and most ancient tradition. Italian archaeologists who have studied 5,500 year-old amphorae, which were excavated in 1930 in the village of Erime and kept in boxes in the Archaeological Museum in Nicosia, discovered traces of tartaric acid which is a basic component of wine. This is the oldest sample that has ever been found in the Mediterranean.

The wine scene has changed significantly in recent decades, compared with the past where the vineyards were cultivated everywhere, regardless of the soil and climate of the area and all varieties were used for wine production, irrespective of whether they were grape varieties or not.

> Italian archaeologists who have studied 5500 year-old amphorae, which were excavated in 1930 in the village of Erime and kept in boxes in the Archaeological Museum in Nicosia, discovered traces of tartaric acid which is a basic component of wine.

Since Cyprus' accession to the European Union in 2004, the wine sector has been significantly upgraded. A new wine map has been created and a legal framework was defined for all categories of wine products and areas where wines with geographical indication and also wines with a protected designation of origin could be produced. Moreover, in recent years, a rapid development of wineries with a close proximity to the wine regions was observed. Currently, apart from the four main wineries, approximately fifty modern and local wineries have been developed by private initiative in the Cyprus countryside, having as a result the configuration of Cypriot wine production as well as the contribution to local development and to the creation of a new wine culture.

Another positive factor that contributes to the overall enhancement of the wine sector is the fact that winegrowers have realised that their vines need more care and also modern cultivation practices in order to produce quality grapes. They have accepted that wineries are not necessarily competitors but collaborators in this difficult task.

Recently, a concerted effort began to restructure and convert vineyards so that several forgotten indigenous varieties, which were scattered in old vineyards, will become known again. From the red varieties the "Maratheftiko" is distinguished and can

The Cyprus Wine Museum in Erime, Pafos district.

be classified as a high and noble variety compared to the white variety "Xynisteri" which stands out for its uniqueness.

In order to support and develop viticulture and winemaking, in 2006, the Wine Products Council began to hold the Annual Wine Competition in Cyprus based on international standards and in accordance with the terms and requirements of the *Organization Internationale de la Vigne et du Vin (OIV)*. The competition is a celebration of the newest achievements of local wine makers and provides a challenge for further enhancement in the years to come. It receives extensive media coverage and has proved to be beneficial in creating awareness for the high quality of Cypriot wine and the accomplishments of the wine producers.

> The most famous of all Cypriot wines is the sweet wine «Commandaria», which has been produced on the island for centuries now.

The competition, being of high international standards, is held under the patronage of the OIV.

The most famous of all Cypriot wines is the sweet wine «Commandaria», which has been produced on the island for centuries now. All the stages of production, apart from the ageing, take place in a specified area which comprises of 14 communities and it is only here that this famous wine with its unique colour and smooth taste can be produced.

Many wineries have been developed by private initiative.

The interior of the
Cyprus Wine Museum,
Erime, Pafos district.